(Nolan & Haley) Alt. Dis. Res. NS-

ALTERNATIVE DISPUTE RESOLUTION
IN A NUTSHELL

By

JACQUELINE M. NOLAN-HALEY
Associate Clinical Professor of Law
Fordham University, School of Law

WEST GROUP

1992

COPYRIGHT © 1992 By WEST PUBLISHING CO.
610 Opperman Drive
P.O. Box 64526
St. Paul, MN 55164–0526

Library of Congress Cataloging-in-Publication Data

Nolan–Haley, Jacqueline M., 1949–
    Alternative dispute resolution in a nutshell / by Jacqueline M. No-
lan–Haley.
        p.   cm. — (Nutshell series)
    Includes index.
    ISBN 0–314–00781–4
    1. Dispute resolution (Law)—United States. I. Title. II. Series.
KF9084.Z9N65   1992
347.73'9—dc20
[347.3079]   92–10940
                                                                  CIP

ISBN 0–314–00781–4

(Nolan–Haley) Alt.Dis.Res. NS
3rd Reprint–1999

To Peggy and Joe

*

To Peggy and Joe

PREFACE

My goal in writing this book is to help law students understand a wide variety of approaches to resolving legal disputes and to encourage them to view litigation, not as the norm, but simply as one means of resolving legal disputes.

I am grateful to Fordham Law School for its financial support through summer grants, to John D. Feerick, the Dean of Fordham Law School for his support and encouragement and to my colleagues who generously gave of their time reading portions of this manuscript and offering helpful suggestions: Jim Boskey, Jim Haley, Cathy Cronin–Harris, Gail Hollister, Carol Liebman, Rosemary Page and Maria Volpe. Students, Scott Fitzgerald, Jeff Hill, Lori Geldzahler and Adam Dubow were helpful with research and many thanks go to Eddie Didona for his skillful and patient technical assistance. Finally a special word of gratitude goes to Jim, Martina and Andrew Haley, for putting up with me while I wrote this book.

JACQUELINE M. NOLAN-HALEY

New York, NY
May 1992

*

V

ACKNOWLEDGMENTS

The following authors and publishers gave me permission to reprint excerpts from copyright material. I gratefully acknowledge their assistance.

Chapter 2

American Bar Association, Model Rules of Professional Conduct and Model Code of Professional Responsibility. Copyright by the ABA. All rights reserved. Reprinted by permission of the American Bar Association.

Lax and Sebenius, The Manager As Negotiator: Bargaining for Cooperation and Competitive Gain 31, 32 (1986). Copyright © 1986 by David A. Lax and James K. Sebenius. Reprinted by permission of Macmillan Publishing Company, a Division of Macmillan, Inc.

G. Williams, Legal Negotiation and Settlement 22–24, (1983). Reprinted by permission of the West Publishing Company.

Brazil, The Attorney as Victim: Towards More Candor About the Psychological Price Tag of Litigation Practice, 3 J. of the Legal Profession 107, 112 (1978).

White, Machiavelli and the Bar: Ethical Limitations on Lying in Negotiation, 1980 Am.B. Foundation Res.J. 926.

Chapter 3

Nolan–Haley & Volpe, Teaching Mediation As A Lawyering Role, 39 J. Legal Ed. 571 (1989).

Fuller, Mediation—Its Forms and Functions, 44 S.Cal.L.Rev. 305, 308, 327 (1971), reprinted with the permission of the *Southern California Law Review.*

Silbey & Merry, Mediator Settlement Strategies, 8 Law & Policy 7, 19–22, 25 (1986). Reprinted with permission from Basil Blackwell Limited.

Society of Professionals in Dispute Resolution (SPIDR), Report of Committee on Law and Public Policy on Mandatory ADR Programs (1991). This report was produced under a grant from the National Institute for Dispute Resolution.

American Bar Association, Standards of Practice for Lawyer Mediators in Family Disputes (Adopted by the House of Delegates of the ABA, 1984). Copyright by the ABA. All rights reserved. Reprinted with permission.

National Institute of Dispute Resolution (NIDR) Dispute Resolution Forum 9, 10 (May 1989).

American Bar Association, Model Rules of Professional Conduct and Model Code of Professional Responsibility. Rule 2.2 excerpted from the Model Rules of Professional Conduct and EC5–20 excerpted from the Model Code of Professional Responsibility, copyrighted by the American Bar Association. All rights reserved. Reprinted with permission.

Association of the Bar of the City of New York, Ethics Opinion, Committee on Professional and Judicial Ethics, Inquiry Reference No. 80–23.

American Arbitration Association, Commercial Mediation Rules as amended and in effect October 1, 1987.

Wigmore's Evidence in Trials at Common Law, Vol. 8, (McNaughton Revision), 527. Reprinted with permission of Little, Brown and Co.

Society of Professionals in Dispute Resolution (SPIDR), Ethical Standards of Professional Responsibility for the Society of Professionals in Dispute Resolution, adopted by the Board of Directors, June 2, 1986.

Chapter 4

American Arbitration Association, Commercial Arbitration Rules: Demand for Arbitration (Form).

Code of Ethics for Arbitrators in Commercial Disputes.

Uniform Arbitration Act. This Act has been reprinted through the permission of the National Conference of Commissioners on Uniform State Laws, and copies of the Act may be ordered from them at a nominal cost at 676 North St. Clair

Street, Suite 1700, Chicago, Illinois 60611, (312) 915–0195.

Restatement of the Law, 2nd, Judgments, Section 84, p. 286. Copyright © 1982 by the American Law Institute. Reprinted with the permission of the American Law Institute.

Chapter 6

American Arbitration Association, Mini-Trial Procedures.

McGovern, Toward A Functional Approach for Managing Complex Litigation, 53 U.Chi.L.Rev. 440, 459 (1986).

OUTLINE

OUTLINE

Appendices

XVII*

Contents

TABLE OF CASES

References are to Pages

TABLE OF CASES

ALTERNATIVE DISPUTE RESOLUTION

IN A NUTSHELL

*

CHAPTER 1

INTRODUCTION

I. OVERVIEW

The traditional legal response to a dispute between parties has been for a lawyer for one of the parties to initiate the litigation process by filing a complaint or motion. Most lawyers who graduated from law school before the mid-seventies would probably choose this option instinctively. Many law students would also probably choose this approach simply because in the majority of law school classrooms the litigation process is assumed to be the appropriate means of resolving a client's legal problems. Law is studied chiefly through the analysis of appellate cases, all of which began with the filing of a complaint, motion or petition. When we add to this the television mystique of People's Court and Perry Mason, it is not surprising that much of the public and many lawyers think that the way to solve problems is by bringing suit.

The chief purpose of this book is to disabuse you of the "one size fits all" litigation mentality and to help you appreciate *alternative* dispute resolution (ADR). ADR is an umbrella term which refers generally to alternatives to court adjudication of

1

disputes such as negotiation, mediation, arbitration, mini-trial and summary jury trial. Even though some of the "alternatives" such as negotiation, mediation and arbitration, have been practiced for hundreds of years, they have achieved a new familiarity today as part of the ADR movement.

This book does not blindly promote the use of alternatives to the traditional litigation process. Rather, the goal is for lawyers to understand a wide variety of dispute resolution mechanisms, including litigation, so that they can help clients choose the process which fits their clients' needs. The client's choice of process may not necessarily correspond to the ego needs of the attorney.

It is certainly not possible in this book to catalogue, let alone describe, every ADR procedure. Instead, the focus is on presenting the major processes of alternative dispute resolution—negotiation, mediation and arbitration as well as some well-known hybrids of these processes such as the summary jury trial and the mini-trial. The study of ADR is an on-going, active process and will continue to develop as long as creative lawyering exists.

II. WHY STUDY ADR?

Studying ADR will help you to be a better lawyer. Most Americans who can afford to, consult a lawyer first when they believe they have been wronged. A lawyer's counseling, therefore, plays an important role in whether a party asserts a claim or brings a dispute into the public arena. If a lawyer decides that there is a legitimate claim and advises the client to proceed, the question becomes—what process should the client use to resolve the particular dispute?

For law students to focus exclusively on the litigation process is like medical students studying only surgery as a means of curing illness. Of course, that is not what medical students do. They study an extensive range of subjects for the treatment and cure of illnesses. Law students too must extend their problem-solving focus beyond the litigation arena. The legal community's failure to do this for so long may be part of the reason for so much congestion in the civil justice system.

Law students cannot afford to ignore developments in ADR as many of these processes become institutionalized within the judicial system in court-annexed programs. Law students must understand ADR processes and develop the skills which are necessary to use them. It is important to learn to identify the factors which make a particular method the process of choice. If for example, there is a need to preserve an on-going relationship between the parties, litigation might not be appropriate since many relationships are terminated in the litigation process. Instead, the mediation process should be considered because it is known to work well where parties have an on-going or prior relationship. On the other hand, if a legal precedent is desirable, litigation may be more appropriate.

A useful way to enhance your process skills is to keep a conflict journal. Make entries on a regular basis about disputes or conflicts you experience and then critically reflect on how you responded. How do you typically resolve conflicts? Through confrontation? Avoidance? Problem-solving? Would other methods be more appropriate? This process of critical self-reflection is what good lawyering is all about. Learn from your experiences.

III. BACKGROUND OF THE AL-TERNATIVE DISPUTE RES-OLUTION MOVEMENT

ADR assumed the attributes of a law reform movement in the early nineteen seventies when many observers in the legal and academic communities began to have serious concerns about the negative effects of increased litigation. Legislation enacted in the nineteen sixties granted a broad range of individual protections from consumer to civil rights. The search for redress of those rights through the legal system, however, was becoming a complex exercise. People began to look for alternatives to the court adjudication of disputes as court congestion, high legal costs and waiting for your day in court became a way of life for Americans who encountered the judicial system either voluntarily or involuntarily.

One well known effort in the search for alternatives occurred in 1976 when former Chief Justice Warren Burger convened the Roscoe E. Pound Conference on the Causes of Popular Dissatisfaction with the Administration of Justice (Pound Conference) in Saint Paul, Minnesota. Academics, members of the judiciary, and public interest lawyers joined together to find new ways of dealing with disputes. Some of the papers which emerged from this conference such as Professor Frank Sander's classic, "Varieties of Dispute Resolution," formed the basic understanding of dispute resolution today.

"Isn't there a better way" asked former Chief Justice Burger and the alternatives movement was officially off and running. The organized bar officially recognized the ADR movement in 1976 when the American Bar Association established a Special Committee on Minor Disputes which has now become the Special Committee on Dispute Resolution. Most state and federal bar associations now have ADR committees. Law schools have gradually been adding ADR to the curriculum and now the majority of law schools offer one or more ADR courses or specialized courses in areas such as mediation and negotiation. Several law reviews are devoted solely to the study of alternative dispute resolution. Similar developments have occurred in graduate and business schools.

In the last decade we have seen an enormous amount of study by cultural anthropologists, sociologists and lawyers on the kinds of disputes that are resolved and how they are resolved and those disputes that are not resolved. The late law professor Lon Fuller invited the legal community to consider ways of resolving "polycentric" problems which have interconnected issues and which, therefore, do not easily lend themselves to resolution through the "all or nothing" approach of adjudication. Fuller offered as an example of a "polycentric" problem, the story of a wealthy testator who bequeathed a collection of paintings in equal parts to two museums. The adjudication process would have been totally inappropriate to resolve the issue in this case because it would simply result in a winner and a loser and therefore, fail to address the interconnected issue of each museum's interest. Thus, for the first time, the legal community began to look thoughtfully at the *process* by which disputes are resolved.

In 1976 Professor Frank Sander proposed the idea of a multidoor courthouse where individual disputes would be matched to appropriate processes such as mediation, arbitration, fact finding or malpractice screening panels. The American Bar Association adopted his idea and established three multidoor courthouses in Houston, Texas, Tulsa, Oklahoma and the District of Columbia. The success of these programs has led other courts to begin similar programs.

Over the last decade we have seen the beginning of a systematic implementation of ADR in the legal system. Judges often order parties to participate in summary jury trials. Court rules require parties to arbitrate in specified categories of cases such as medical malpractice. In some courts, parties are required to try the mediation process before being permitted to have a trial.

Mandatory ADR raises a host of public policy issues. Some critics have charged that in our eagerness to adopt alternatives to litigation we risk losing the protection of the rule of law. Other critics are concerned that some forms of ADR, such as court-annexed mediation, may become a lesser standard of justice for the poor who cannot afford attorneys. Professor Owen Fiss suggests that enthusiastic adoption of ADR minimizes the importance of lawsuits in responding to public policy issues.

In the private sector, ADR has become a cottage industry of sorts. Private ADR businesses offer a wide range of services ranging from private judging to mediation. Retired judges often act as neutrals to assist in resolving disputes. Many law firms have developed ADR departments and offer similar services to the private providers.

Federal ADR legislation has expanded significantly. One of the most comprehensive statutes, the Civil Justice Reform Act of 1990, 28 U.S.C.A. § 1 requires every federal district court to develop a "civil justice expense and delay reduction plan" (EDRP). The purpose of such plans is "to facilitate deliberate adjudication of civil cases on the merits, monitor discovery, improve litigation management, and ensure just, speedy, and inexpensive resolutions of civil disputes." The Act recommends six methods for courts to use in developing EDRPs, one of which is referring appropriate cases "to alternative dispute resolution programs ... including mediation, minitrial, and summary jury trial."

The Negotiated Rulemaking Act of 1990, 5 U.S.C.A. § 581, authorizes the use of negotiated rulemaking as an alternative to adversarial rulemaking in federal agencies. Under the scheme established by the Act, parties who will be significantly affected by an agency rule, participate in the development of the rule.

The Administrative Dispute Resolution Act of 1990, 5 U.S.C.A. § 581, requires all federal agencies to develop policies on the voluntary use of alternative dispute resolution. The purpose of the Act is "to offer a prompt, expert, and inexpensive means of resolving disputes as an alternative to litigation in federal courts." In its findings, Congress stated that "the availability of a wide range of dispute resolution procedures, and an increased understanding of the most effective use of such procedures, will enhance the operation of the Government and better serve the public."

One thing that we have realized is that there are limits to the judicial process. High legal costs and long delays put a damper on the exercise of an individual's right to go to court. Once a case is in court, it is the judges and lawyers who are the major participants while the affected party often sits on the sidelines. A remedy will be fashioned by a neutral third party, applying a rule of law. Usually, it will be a money judgment. The judicial approach does not consider the affected party's feelings and allows little room for other values such as an apology to the malpractice victim or substitute employment for the injured worker.

On the other hand, ADR remedies are tailored to meet individual needs. The use of ADR personalizes what federal judge John Noonan calls the "faces and masks of the law." People's names and feelings are important in a process such as mediation. Private as well as public agendas are important in negotiation. The parties' notion of fairness is important in structuring an arbitration. Advising a client to apologize may be just as crucial as counseling her to file or defend a lawsuit.

Your study of ADR should be closely connected to developing your own theory of lawyering. What are the values which bring you to law school? What does it mean to be a lawyer at the beginning of the twenty first century? Are you simply an advocate for clients? For a cause? What do you hope to accomplish by being a lawyer?

An ADR lawyering perspective goes beyond the bounds of advocacy to help clients help themselves. Implementing the theory of problem solving through such processes as negotiation, and mediation, advances that goal. Lawyers can educate their clients about the range of choices of ways to accomplish their goals. The choice of process may depend upon who is doing the disputing—institutional disputants such as corporations, unions and government agencies, special interest groups, or individuals, and what is being disputed—individual rights, property rights, constitutional rights, etc.

Lawyers should also consider the standards by which they help their clients arrive at solutions. How do lawyers insure the accuracy of information in ADR processes where parties take no oath to tell the truth? How do lawyers know that the outcome of an ADR method is a fair result? In many respects, the questions are more important than the answers.

BIBLIOGRAPHY

Fiss, *"Against Settlement,"* 93 Yale L.J. 1073 (1984); Fuller, *"The Forms and Limits of Adjudication,"* 92 Harvard Law Review, 353 (1979).

Goldberg, Green and Sander, Chapter 1 in *Dispute Resolution* (1985).

Sander, *"Varieties of Dispute Resolution,"* 70 F.R.D. 111 (1976).

CHAPTER 2

NEGOTIATION

I. INTRODUCTION

Negotiation is a fundamental skill that all lawyers need. Corporate lawyers negotiate business deals. Government lawyers negotiate with administrative agencies. Even trial lawyers must negotiate because more often than not, the transaction costs of going to trial outweigh the benefits of a courthouse "victory." Thus, the vast majority of all civil and criminal cases are settled through negotiation.

The study of negotiation involves an analysis of process skills, procedural requirements, and professional responsibility standards as well as substantive law. If an agreement is reached in negotiation, the lawyer is concerned with its validity as well as the appropriateness of the agreement to serve the client's needs. Understanding how that result was reached involves the study of process, procedure, ethical norms and behavior.

The notion that somehow negotiators are born and not made is false. Negotiation is not simply an intuitive process. You can learn theories of bargaining, develop strategies and then practice and perfect your negotiation skills.

11

Legal negotiation differs from other types of negotiation because it involves lawyers acting as agents representing clients. The agency relationship adds a collaborative dynamic to the negotiation process. Prior to the actual negotiation, the lawyer works with the client to help determine the client's particular goals and objectives. Lawyers must develop an in-depth understanding of the client's aims. During the negotiation, the lawyer-negotiator must keep the client informed of what is going on and also has the responsibility of protecting the client's interests. A lawyer is involved in the negotiation process not to accomplish her goals but to serve her client. Lawyers, therefore, must assist clients in defining their goals for a particular negotiation. At the completion of the negotiation, the client, not the lawyer, decides ultimately whether to accept a particular settlement offer. The American Bar Association's Model Rules of Professional Conduct make this clear: "a lawyer shall abide by a client's decision whether to accept an offer of settlement on a matter." Rule 1.2(a) (1983).

The importance of negotiation skills in the dispute resolution universe cannot be overemphasized. Negotiation is the foundational skill for successful implementation of many ADR processes, such as mediation, the mini-trial and summary jury trial. A theoretical and practical understanding of negotiation enhances the lawyer's effectiveness in these procedures. Mediation, an extension of negotiation, is a process in which a neutral third party, the mediator, helps negotiating parties to reach a mutually acceptable agreement. The mediator who does not understand the dynamics of negotiation is of dubious assistance to the parties in the mediation process. The same is true for a lawyer who represents clients in a minitrial or summary jury trial. The post-hearing settlement talks may be more informed following these ADR proceedings, but they will not be effective if the lawyer does not know how to make the negotiation process work effectively for her client.

II. DEFINITIONS AND CONCEPTS

Negotiation may be generally defined as a consensual bargaining process in which parties attempt to reach agreement on a disputed or potentially disputed matter. The whole point of parties negotiating is to achieve an advantage which is not possible by unilateral action. Negotiation differs from other methods of dispute resolution in the degree of autonomy experienced by the disputing parties who are attempting to reach agreement without the intervention of third parties such as judges, arbitrators or mediators.

A. DISPUTE AND TRANSACTIONAL NEGOTIATION

Negotiations may be classified as either dispute or transactional negotiations. In planning for a negotiation, lawyers must initially determine which type is involved. *Transactional* negotiation involves parties planning for a future event such as licensing a copyright agreement, drafting an employment contract or a long-term lease or other similar long-term goals. In a *dispute* negotiation the parties are in conflict over an event which has occurred—the contract which was breached, the patent which was infringed, the personal injury which was sustained. The issues in dispute negotiation are often susceptible to resolution by a third party such as a judge or arbitrator, while, in transactional negotiation, the issues are resolved by the parties themselves. It is not surprising then that dispute negotiation is often a prelude to litigation between the parties.

Strategic planning will obviously differ depending upon how a negotiation is classified. If preserving a relationship is important to the client in a transactional negotiation, for example, then any tactics which harm that relationship would be inappropriate. The lawyer-negotiator would attempt to avoid an unfavorable outcome in a transaction negotiation in order to preserve the underlying deal. In some cases, however, a failed transactional negotiation not only results in a loss of the bargain, but can even lead to litigation.

This is what occurred in *Hoffman v. Red Owl Stores, Inc.,* (1965), a case familiar to many first year law students because of its importance in common law developments in the law of promissory estoppel. In a series of detailed transactions, Joseph Hoffman and his wife negotiated with agents of the Red Owl stores to establish Hoffman as a franchise operator of a Red Owl store in Chilton, Wisconsin. Red Owl agents made representations to Hoffman that, if he fulfilled several conditions, he would become a franchise operator. The negotiations terminated between the parties when Hoffman informed Red Owl that he objected to some terms in their proposal. What result? Not only did the transaction negotiation fail, i.e. Hoffman never received the franchise, but extensive litigation ensued over alleged promises made during the negotiation.

B.   DISTRIBUTIVE AND INTEGRATIVE BARGAINING

Negotiation may be further classified into *distributive* or *integrative* bargaining situations. *Distributive* bargaining exists where the parties believe that there are limited resources to divide. Individual, rather than joint gain, is sought. Typically, the negotiator engages in *positional* bargaining, claiming a particular position and arguing for it throughout the negotiation process. To insure that the position is realized, the negotiator would usually take an extreme position, make few concessions and ultimately arrive at the desired position.

There is a *zero-sum* dimension to this bargaining—more for me automatically means less for you. Consider a simple example where S, a second year law student, wants to sell her first year law books for the highest possible price. B, a first year law student, wants to pay the lowest possible price for the books. The negotiations between S and B over the price of the books can be described as a *zero-sum* situation where gain by S comes at the expense of B.

In an *integrative bargaining* situation, the parties' goals are not necessarily at odds with each other so that mutual gain is possible and oftentimes, desirable. Integrative bargaining usually involves multiple issues so that it is possible to develop several alternative mutually beneficial solutions. The negotiator would engage in *interest* bargaining and focus on the underlying needs and concerns which support a particular position. The negotiator explores those interests and seeks opportunities to develop responsive solutions.

Wherever possible, negotiators should try to transform the context of bargaining into integrative situations. Consider the following integrative approaches to negotiation.

Example 1

A Transaction Negotiation

Eastern University wishes to recruit Professor X, a national expert in governmental affairs to develop its political science department. Professor X and her husband, a chemist, currently teach at Western University. The recruitment has the potential for deadlock because of Professor X's salary demands. Eastern has offered her a salary of

$75,000.00 but Professor X claims she would only leave Western University for a salary of $95,-000.00. Eastern is not in a position to pay this salary. Hefty budget cuts have affected all departments of the university and it is unclear whether the political science department will receive outside funding this year. Additionally, the highest paid professor in the political science department receives a salary of $85,000.00 so that even if funds were available, it might not be appropriate to bring in a newcomer at a higher salary.

At first glance this looks like a *distributive* bargaining situation because the sole disputed issue is the amount of money which Professor X will receive. It is possible, however, to consider the opportunities for joint gain and transform this into an *integrative bargaining* situation. If Eastern University and Professor X examine their goals, they would probably learn that Eastern wants to establish a first class political science department while Professor X is interested in establishing a national reputation in political science. Working collaboratively, they are better able to achieve those goals. If Professor X's salary demands are based on financial concerns, then additional items could be included with the Eastern's offer: assistance with locating a consulting or teaching position for her husband, health care benefits, housing assistance, travel grants, child care, an endowed chair etc. If scholarship is a concern, then items such as early sabbatical leave, lighter teaching load and additional research assistants could be discussed. While these are all separate issues, it may possible to resolve them interdependently, so that the result would then be a non *zero-sum* situation where both parties can gain by negotiating a settlement on all items together.

Example 2
A Dispute Negotiation

The tenants in an urban apartment complex suffered serious interruptions of services during a strike by maintenance workers. After conditions became close to intolerable as rats, roaches, and other vermin ran rampant, the tenants started a rent strike. The landlord demanded that the tenants pay their rent and threatened legal action. The tenants hired an attorney and agreed that if a case were brought to court by the landlord that they would all testify to the above-stated facts.

Consider the type of negotiation process which could take place in this case. The landlord and tenant's lawyers could view this as a distributive bargaining problem and posture the bargaining so that it becomes an adversarial, win-lose proposition. More money for the landlord means less money for the tenants or vice-versa.

If the negotiation failed, however, the parties would end up in court. Both sides would then risk a total loss. Litigation would only prolong the bad conditions in the building (assuming the maintenance strike continued) and the landlord's need for the rent money. The publicity from the litigation could be harmful to both the landlord and the tenants.

Alternatively, the lawyers could help their clients focus on the opportunities which exist for joint gain, thereby transforming this negotiation into an integrative bargaining context. Both the landlord and tenants could explore ways to furnish the services until the maintenance strike ended. The tenants could agree to pay the rent with an abatement until the repairs were made. Both sides had much to gain from a speedy resolution of the issue. The tenants hopefully would have the necessary repairs made to their building and the landlord would receive rent money with which he could arrange to have the repairs made and make the mortgage payments.

III. APPROACHES TO NEGOTIATION

A. IN GENERAL

The literature on legal negotiation identifies two major orientations which describe how lawyers generally negotiate: adversarial and problem-solving. Within each orientation, lawyers will adopt specific strategies, tactics and styles. The early writings on legal negotiation focused primarily on the adversarial approach to negotiation. As the study of the legal negotiation process becomes more sophisticated, however, there is a growing recognition that the problem-solving approach may be more efficient and that it may result in more mutually satisfactory outcomes. Of course, a lawyer's decision to adopt an adversarial or problem-solving approach depends upon the context and goals of the particular negotiation.

1. Adversarial Approach

The primary goal of the lawyer who engages in adversarial negotiation is to maximize individual gain. To achieve that goal, the negotiator engages primarily in positional bargaining, a strategy which has been described by Fisher and Ury as one in which the negotiator adopts a particular position, advances arguments to support that position, makes some concessions and finally reaches a compromise solution. The adversarial negotiator stays close to her client's positions and maneuvers and structures the negotiation process so that it moves through those positions. The journey of the adversarial negotiator is, therefore, closely mapped out between her client's bottom line and stated position.

In *The Manager as Negotiator,* Lax and Sebenius characterize adversarial, competitive negotiators as the "value claimers" for whom "[T]he object of negotiation is to convince the other guy that he wants what you have to offer much more than you want what he has; moreover, you have all the time in the world while he is up against pressing deadlines." The adversarial negotiator usually perceives the issues in negotiation as distributive; she assumes that there is only one prize in the official jackpot and firmly believes that her job for her client is to get that prize. The negotiation process is viewed as a zero-sum game, at the end of which there will be a winner and a loser.

The adversarial negotiator may use competitive or cooperative tactics to win this game. Professor Gerald Williams' empirical study of lawyer's negotiating behavior shows that the goals of the effective competitive negotiator include: maximizing settlement for their clients; obtaining profitable fees for themselves; and, outmaneuvering their opponents. They are perceived as dominating, forceful, aggressive, tough, arrogant, and uncooperative. Their strategy is to make high opening demands and few concessions. They use threats, are willing to stretch the facts in favor of their clients' positions, stick to their positions, and are parsimonious with information about the case.

The whole purpose of this behavior is to create substantial doubt in the mind of the opposing negotiator about the validity of her position. The opposing negotiator may lose confidence and arrive at a less than satisfactory solution for her client.

Cooperative negotiators use radically different tactics to achieve the same end as the competitive negotiators. According to Professor Williams' study, the effective cooperative negotiator had the following characteristics: conducting self ethically; maximizing settlement for client; getting a fair settlement; meeting client's needs; avoiding litigation; and maintaining or establishing a good personal relationship with the opponent. These motivational objectives were observed in attorneys who were perceived as fair, objective, reasonable, logical, and willing to move from their established positions. Professor Williams' study showed that the highest proportion of effective negotiators were in the cooperative category.

2. Problem–Solving Approach

A problem-solving orientation in negotiation focuses on the opportunities for joint, rather than individual, gain. The negotiator views the dispute or transaction as a mutual problem which has the potential of being resolved to the parties mutual satisfaction. It is not just a "game" to be won. The problem-solving approach usually functions in an integrative (multiple issue), rather than a distributive (single issue) context.

Lax and Sebenius characterize problem-solving negotiators as "value creators" who "advocate exploring and cultivating shared interests in substance, in maintaining a working relationship, in having a pleasant nonstrident negotiation process, in mutually held norms or principles, and even in reaching agreement at all." Many of the characteristics of the cooperative negotiator in Professor Williams' study could apply to the problem-solving negotiator.

Professor Carrie Menkel–Meadow describes the methodology used in the problem-solving negotiation model in her seminal article, "Toward Another View of Legal Negotiation: The Structure of Problem–Solving"—first, through extensive negotiation planning and brainstorming, the parties' underlying needs and objectives are identified; second, solutions which respond to those needs are formulated. In *Getting to Yes,* Fisher and Ury propose a bargaining model for using the problem-solving approach to negotiation. The authors suggest that as an alternative to the competitiveness of positional bargaining, negotiators engage in interest-based bargaining. This model requires that the negotiator distinguish the issues or problems from the parties involved in the dispute, and then concentrate on responding to the parties' underlying needs and interests rather than their stated positions.

Getting to Yes has been criticized for concentrating too much attention on the integrative aspects of bargaining and failing to deal with the difficulty of responding to distributive issues. In a more recent book, *Getting Past No: Negotiating With Difficult People,* Ury responds to some of these criticisms and discusses what to do when the other negotiator refuses to adopt a problem-solving approach to negotiation.

What approach should the negotiating attorney adopt? Is it ever possible or reasonable to adopt a single approach? Probably not. Lax and Sebenius argue that the processes of value creating and value claiming are both present in every negotiation. At some point in the negotiation process, the resources which are available to the parties become fixed and must be divided among competing interests. The inherent tension in every negotiation lies in making choices about the approach to use in determining how those resources will be divided. Behavior that makes the negotiator a successful value creator causes the same negotiator to become vulnerable when dealing with the value claimer. By the same token, the behavior necessary to claim value is counterproductive in creating value.

In every negotiation, lawyers must consciously consider whether an adversarial or problem-solving approach best serves their clients' interests. Thus, working collaboratively with their clients, lawyers must first determine the goals they hope to achieve in a negotiation. Whether the goal is to sever a relationship or to cement one, to open a deal or to close one, a conscious choice must be made about the appropriate negotiating approach.

NEGOTIATION APPROACHES		
ADVERSARIAL		PROBLEM–SOLVING
Goal:	maximize self gain	seeks joint gain
Behavior:	competitive positional bargaining	facilitative interest bargaining
Perception of issues:	distributive zero-sum win-lose	integrative non-zero sum win-win

B. NEGOTIATION APPROACHES
IN PRACTICE

Problem

A owns a patent on a product (x), which could cure tuberculosis and for which there is a very large world market. A does not plan to develop or market (x). Instead, A is conducting clinical tests and awaiting government approval to sell a different, unpatented product (y), which also cures tuberculosis. This may take one to two more years. B already has government approval and has begun selling product (x) as a cure for tuberculosis without A's consent. B's sales of product (x) infringe A's patent. A tells B that his sale of product (x) infringes A's patent and warns B not to continue making, using or selling the product. B refuses.

Under an adversarial, competitive model, A might say—get off the market and stop selling my product (x) or I sue. This of course is classic, positional bargaining. To avoid a very costly lawsuit which could result in an injunction against B's future sales, damages for B's sales to date and punitive damages for B's willful infringement of A's patent, B might agree to stop selling product (x) if A would agree not to seek damages for past infringement or punitive damages. A would have given up the potential recovery from B of past damages and punitive damages, to retain the tuberculosis market for himself. The result, however, is that no one is on the market until A's product (y) is approved by the government and a product (x), potentially helpful to C, a tuberculosis patient, is unavailable.

Alternatively, under a problem-solving approach, using interest bargaining, a more beneficial and efficient outcome may be possible. A might say "I will agree to license B to use my patent to sell product (x)." A would benefit by receiving money from B and when A's product (y) reached the market, A would have an overall financial advantage over B. A would have no royalty obligation against the sales of product (y). B on the other hand would pay royalty to A, on all sales of B's product (x). A and B, however, would be permitted to sell their products and C, the potential tuberculosis patient, would be well served by a likely lower price (because of price competition between A and B for market share) and by a choice of two products from which to choose.

IV. STAGES OF THE NEGOTIATION PROCESS

Negotiation approaches will vary depending upon a number of variables—the client's goals, the subject matter, the personalities of the parties involved and the negotiator's individual preferences. Negotiating with your children is obviously quite different from negotiating with your clients. Before adopting an approach to negotiation, it is important to understand how a legal negotiation operates. The following elements constitute the generic negotiation process:

1. Planning and analysis
2. Exchanging information
3. Concessions and compromise
4. Reaching agreement

Negotiation is a fluid process and these stages do not necessarily occur in linear fashion. It is quite possible, for example, that a lawyer-negotiator may exchange substantial information about the value of a case before deciding on a planning approach to a particular negotiation. Or, after exchanging information with opposing counsel, the attorney may modify her initial approach. Consider the hypothetical case of a lawyer who represents a former marathon runner in an orthopedic malpractice case. The client's big toe was so severely damaged by the orthopedic surgeon in a bunionectomy that the client will not be able to run competitively in any future marathons. During the initial planning stages, the client tells the lawyer that he is very angry, that he is nervous and tense all the time because his sense of self-esteem was wrapped up in his running. Now, money is the bottom line for him and he wants no less than half a million dollars from the orthopedic surgeon. The client asks the lawyer to engage in aggressive advocacy. After deposing the orthopedic surgeon, the lawyer learns that there are numerous ways to perform a bunionectomy and that the method used by the orthopedic surgeon on her client might even be considered appropriate. The lawyer also learns from her client that instead of running competitively, the client is now race-walking and has already entered two regional competitions.

Given this information, the lawyer-negotiator might well decide that an adversarial approach would be totally inappropriate and probably counterproductive. Competitive strategies might result in deadlock and the case would have to go to trial. Because there are many methods of performing a bunionectomy, there is a more than strong chance that a jury would find no negligence. Even if the jury found the surgeon to be negligent, the fact that the client is still engaged in competitive sports would significantly diminish the amount of damages. The lawyer would then explain all of these considerations to the client and suggest that it would be preferable to adopt a problem-solving approach or at the very least, a cooperative strategy, in the hope of inducing cooperation from the other side.

A. PLANNING AND ANALYSIS

GOALS   OBJECTIVES   STRATEGY   TACTICS

Strategic planning is the key to successful negotiation and maximum time should be invested at this stage of the negotiation process. Just as a good trial lawyer would not dream of beginning a trial without a thorough knowledge of the facts and relevant substantive law and a well-designed strategic plan, neither should the negotiating lawyer.

At the initial planning and analysis stage the lawyer must work collaboratively with the client to identify and prioritize the client's goals. The skills used by lawyers in client interviewing and counseling, such as fact investigation and active listening, will be most helpful in the planning stages.

After learning the facts and the client's goals, the lawyer-negotiator must consider the appropriate method to achieve those goals. Just what does your client want out of this situation? Is money the bottom line or does your client want to establish or maintain a business or other relationship?

In helping the client to identify goals and objectives, the lawyer-negotiator should consider how many parties are involved in or affected by the negotiation. This is a critical part of the planning analysis because the negotiation dynamic operates differently in a multi-party, than a two-party situation. Obviously the negotiation of a class action where coalitions may develop will usually be a more complicated process than a negotiation in a two party transaction. In the planning and analysis stage, lawyer-negotiators must also examine whether there are any related transactions which may impact on the instant negotiation. A simple example of this would be representing the seller of a residential home where the buyer's ability to close the transaction depends upon his sale of his home within a six month period.

Throughout the planning and analysis stage, the lawyer should continuously explain all of the parameters of the case as openly as possible so that there can be meaningful involvement by the client who should also have some input on negotiation strategy. This is consistent with the dictates of the Model Rules of Professional Conduct which provide in Rule 1.4(b) that "[a] lawyer shall explain a matter to the extent reasonably necessary to permit the client to make informed decisions regarding the representation." Working collaboratively with the client, the lawyer then maps out specific objectives, a strategic plan and tactical approaches that will achieve the client's desired goals. Ultimately, it will be the client who decides whether or not to accept a settlement proposal.

Clients who are actively involved in the planning and analysis stage of a negotiation are much more likely to be satisfied with the end result and with their lawyer than are clients who are kept in the dark by their lawyers. Consider the case of two clients X and Y who had similar personal injury cases against Z arising out of the same automobile accident. Both X and Y claimed $100,000.00 in damages. However, they each received only $20,-000.00 in settlement. X had several meetings with her lawyer where X helped him understand what was important to her in the case and the lawyer explained what was likely to happen. X and her lawyer talked about how best to pursue those goals. Y's lawyer, on the other hand, had one meeting with her and wrote her one letter in three years which told her to come to a deposition. At the end of three years both X and Y receive a letter from their respective attorneys which said "Congratulations, I have just settled your case for $20,000.00." Who do you think will be the more satisfied client?

Planning checklist

1. learn underlying facts of dispute
2. determine whether additional information is needed
3. determine weakest aspects of client's case—vulnerability points and the strongest aspects of client's case
4. determine client's goals and objectives
5. determine whether the client wants to participate in the negotiation
6. research and review relevant law
7. determine alternatives to reaching a negotiated agreement—e.g., the deal will be lost; a lawsuit will be filed
8. issues analysis: distributive or integrative
9. decide upon initial strategy and tactics (subject to change depending upon opposing counsel's behavior)

10. determine what information to give the opposing party

B. EXCHANGING INFORMATION

The information exchange begins the "getting to
know you" part of the negotiation. Lawyers meet
each other through phone calls, letters or personal
contact. Each party offers an initial assessment of
the case. How lawyers react to each other may
determine the future of the negotiation in terms of
the strategy and tactics which each side will use.
Will I cooperate? Do I trust this negotiator? Will
she be open with me? What is her reputation for
fairness? Do I want to show that I am tough?

Control over the information acquisition process
is crucial to the success of negotiation. How we
acquire and disclose information will often determine the outcome and efficiency of the negotiation.
Here, it is likely that ethical issues related to
truthfulness and fairness in negotiation may be
raised.

Listening is an important skill to develop in the
information exchange. It is a skill, however, not
easily acquired by many lawyers, who find it difficult to resist the urge to interrupt conversation
with another question. Effective listening can be a
passive experience simply involving moments of
concentrated silence or it can require active participation in summarizing what you have heard from
the other party. Active participatory listening
tells the other party not only that you hear her

story but that you understand the feelings and emotions which are connected with that story. Listening is discussed in more detail in Chapter 3 on mediation.

Generating options

As information is exchanged, parties further explore ways to enlarge the pie both in terms of possible solutions and available resources. What besides money damages would satisfy the client's or opponent's needs? If money damages alone are the priority, should they be paid in a lump sum or as part of a structured settlement? This exploration is an on-going process throughout the negotiation.

First Offer

A crucial part of the information exchange is the first offer. Who makes it? What are its contents? When should it be made? The negotiation literature is replete with advice about the merits and demerits of making the first offer. Like so many other areas of law, the only general rule with respect to who makes the first offer, is that it depends upon the circumstances. In some competitive bargaining situations, it may not matter who makes the first offer because opening offers are usually quite extreme and therefore less likely to establish a credible zone of bargaining. In other situations however, a major advantage of making the first offer lies in the offeror's potential control of the outer limits of the bargaining zone. A

negotiator should never make the first offer, however, without a thorough knowledge of the case
because the initial offer may be below the range
within which the case could be settled. For example, in the tuberculosis patent licensing case, discussed earlier, A, looking only to the present market, could offer to settle the patent infringement
dispute by giving a license to B for ten thousand
dollars a year. A has obviously limited the settlement by her initial offer. If the market is likely to
grow rapidly, however, A's opening "present-day"
bid will have cost it dearly over the life of the
patent.

In thinking about the content and range of the
first offer the negotiator should leave room for
maneuvering by the other party. Making the first
offer on a "take it or leave it basis" leaves no
opportunity for the other side to engage in any
semblance of bargaining. This tactic, known as
"Boulwarism," derives from Lemuel R. Boulware
who used the "take it or leave it" technique during
his tenure as vice-president of General Electric
Company during the 1950's. General Electric
avoided working with the union representatives in
the collective bargaining process by going directly
to the workers with what it considered to be fair
and reasonable proposals. Generally, the company's first offer was its final offer. The practice of
bypassing union representatives and going to the
workers with firm first offers was finally held to be
an unfair labor practice by the National Labor
Relations Board because it represented a failure to

bargain in good faith. *N.L.R.B. v. General Electric Co.* (1969).

C. CONCESSIONS AND COMPROMISE

By the time that the legal and factual issues have been distilled, the dispute is sufficiently refined to begin the "give and take" aspect of the negotiation process. Usually there are external factors such as impending deadlines which initiate this movement by the parties. By exchanging concessions, the parties begin to narrow the zone of the dispute. If compromise is reached on at least some of the issues involved, the parties create a good climate which is conducive to a final agreement.

Concessions are a crucial part of the negotiation process and the lawyer who decides to be "up front" and reveal her client's bottom line at the beginning of the negotiation has foreclosed the opportunity to make concessions and thus, cannot really participate in the bargaining process in any meaningful fashion. Professor Gerald Williams' empirical study of lawyers' negotiating behavior shows that making few concessions is one of the characteristics of the competitive negotiator. If opposing counsel does not reciprocate with concessions, caution should be exercised.

Negotiators adopting a cooperative strategy may use the "logrolling" tactic of offering concessions on some issues in exchange for concessions by the other party. Joint gain results because the parties have traded concessions based on their priorities.

D. REACHING AGREEMENT

When the parties finally reach a settlement, then the actual mechanics of the agreement must be worked out. This process demands prudent exercise of the same process skills which produced the agreement because packaging all the details of the final agreement may involve a separate negotiation. The lawyer who drafts the final settlement agreement should always be mindful of contract law principles regarding the validity and effect of settlement agreements and consider whether some type of penalty provisions should be included in the case of noncompliance.

V. ETHICAL ISSUES IN NEGOTIATION

Legal negotiations should be distinguished from market place dealings by the integrity and professionalism of the lawyers who negotiate. This ideal is reflected in the Preamble to the Model Rules of Professional Conduct (Model Rules) adopted by the American Bar Association in 1983: "(a)s a negotiator a lawyer seeks a result advantageous to the client but consistent with the requirements of honest dealings with others." The practice of "honest dealings with others" is most difficult to define with dispute negotiations in on-going litigation. Federal magistrate Wayne Brazil has written of the negative aspects of settlement negctiations:

Some of the most exaggerated and obvious abuses of the litigator's manipulative and deceptive tools take place during settlement negotiations. Occasional melodramatic performances only highlight the somewhat more subtle acts of subterfuge, concealment, and emotional posturing that seem to be the perennial attendants of settlement negotiations. The goal is to manipulate your opponent, through whatever emotional pressures or rational arguments will have the desired effect, into giving your client the best "deal" possible. If that deal happens to coincide with what is fair, fine; but the goal all too frequently is that best "deal," not fairness. Short of bald lying, many attorneys will resort to almost any device that "works" in the settlement process, e.g., appealing to feelings of guilt, pandering to vanities, exploiting fears, generating confusions, and, above all, hiding as many of the damaging balls of evidence as possible.

"The Attorney as Victim: Toward More Candor About the Psychological Price Tag of Litigation Practice," 3 Journal of the Legal Profession 107 (1978).

Negotiating behavior is constrained generally by the substantive law of crimes, torts and contract. For lawyers, there are additional constraints imposed by professional codes, either the Model Code of Professional Responsibility promulgated by the American Bar Association in 1969 or the Model Rules, adopted by a majority of states.

A. TRUTHFULNESS

One of the recurring ethical issues in legal negotiation concerns truthfulness. How much are we
required to reveal? How honest must we be in our
statements? Truthfulness may seem antithetical
to the competitive negotiator who is trying to create doubt in the mind of her opponent about the
validity of her position.

The fundamental tension in this area derives
from two obligations imposed on the negotiating
lawyer: the legal and ethical disclosure requirements of negotiation and the lawyer's duty to protect her client's interests. The reality is that negotiation is essentially a private activity and there
are few, if any, mechanisms to enforce a requirement of truthfulness. Professor James White has
cogently characterized the dilemma:

> If one negotiator lies to another, only by happen-
> stance will the other discover the lie. If the
> settlement is concluded by negotiation, there will
> be no trial, no public testimony by conflicting
> witnesses, and thus no opportunity to examine
> the truthfulness of assertions made during the
> negotiation. Consequently, in negotiation, more
> than in other contexts, ethical norms can proba-
> bly be violated with greater confidence that
> there will not be discovery and punishment.

"Machiavelli and the Bar: Ethical Limitations on
Lying in Negotiation," 1980 Amer. Bar Foundation
Research Journal 926 (1980).

B. MISREPRESENTATION

Where lack of truthfulness in negotiation rises to the level of deliberate misrepresentation, a lawyer may be subject to liability under tort and contract law depending upon the level of deception involved.

The negotiator who deliberately misrepresents a fact, opinion, intention or law so that the opposing negotiator will rely on it, may be liable for fraudulent misrepresentation (*Restatement (Second) of Torts* § 525). For example, a lawyer who deliberately tells her opposing negotiator that her client has only $25,000.00 of liability insurance, when in fact her client has $100,000.00 policy, may be exposed to tort liability if the opposing counsel settles the case for $25,000.00 based on that representation.

What about disclosure requirements? When does a negotiator's silence subject her to liability? There are two situations where a negotiator may incur civil liability for silence. The first is where a negotiator intentionally conceals a material fact or does something that prevents the other party from acquiring the information. The second situation involves failure to disclose where there is a duty to disclose, where for example, there is a fiduciary relationship between the parties.

Contract law also provides redress if there has been a misrepresentation which is either fraudulent or material. (*Restatement (Second) of Contracts,* § 164). In the same example above with the lawyer who misrepresented the amount of her client's liability insurance, the settlement agreement which resulted from that misrepresentation could be set aside.

Both contract and tort law recognize a puffing exception for statements upon which a person would not reasonably rely. For example, in one case, the statements of an auctioneer that "the trucks are in good condition," and "the trucks are ready to work tomorrow" were considered permissible "puffing" even when the same truck broke down shortly after purchase because of a crack in the engine block. *Pell City Wood v. Forke Bros. Auctioneers* (1985).

The lawyer-negotiator is a member of a profession and quite apart from substantive law, lawyer's professional codes govern bluffing, puffing and lying in the negotiation context. Model Rule 4.1, Truthfulness in Statements to Others, describes the extent to which a lawyer must speak the truth in negotiation:

> In the course of representing a client a lawyer shall not knowingly: (a) make a false statement of material fact or law to a third person; or (b) fail to disclose a material fact to a third person when disclosure is necessary to avoid assisting a criminal or fraudulent act by a client ...

Model Rule 4.1 corresponds to EC 7–102(A)(5) under the Code of Professional Responsibility.

The official explanatory comment to Model Rule 4.1 states that:

A lawyer is required to be truthful when dealing with others on a client's behalf, but generally has no affirmative duty to inform an opposing party of relevant facts. A misrepresentation can occur if the lawyer incorporates or affirms a statement of another person that the lawyer knows is false. Misrepresentation can also occur by failure to act.

The Comment then delineates three categories where certain statements are not considered material fact—

Estimates of price or value placed on the subject of a transaction and a party's intentions as to an acceptable settlement of a claim are in this category, and so is the existence of an undisclosed principal except where nondisclosure of the principal would constitute fraud.

A lawyer's professional credibility is at stake in every negotiation situation. If I negotiate with you and you deliberately mislead me, I will have a low level of trust the next time that we negotiate. Even though negotiation is essentially a private activity, the lawyer-negotiator should always conform her conduct to the highest standards of professionalism. In addition to the constraints of substantive law and the ethical codes, the individual lawyer's own sense of professionalism should require the highest aspirations of integrity in the bargaining process. The important thing to remember is that once lost, a lawyer's reputation for honesty and fair dealing is not easily retrieved.

C. THREATS

Making threats is characteristic of a competitive, adversarial bargaining style. Empirical evidence suggests that threats often result in concessions from the other negotiator, which is precisely the result desired by the competitive negotiator. Of course, to have this effect, the threats must be credible. Threats also have an informational function. Depending on the nature of the threat, the opposing negotiator learns the depth of your commitment to your position.

Is making threats consistent with the Model Code's requirement of honest dealings with others? The Model Rules do not address threats in the negotiation context specifically but simply prohibit lawyers from engaging in conduct which adversely reflects on fitness to practice law. Model Rule 8.4(b) and (c) provide:

It is professional misconduct for a lawyer to:

. . .

(b) commit a criminal act that reflects adversely on the lawyer's honesty, trustworthiness or fitness as a lawyer in other respects;

(c) engage in conduct involving dishonesty, fraud, deceit or misrepresentation

Clearly some threats are part of a lawyer's permissible negotiating baggage. "If we can't settle this matter today, we'll go to trial and hear what the judge thinks." "These are my client's settlement figures and either you accept them or we go to the jury." On the other hand, a lawyer who threatens to harm one of the parties in negotiation may be liable under the criminal laws of extortion. A lawyer who threatens to bring criminal charges against a party in the context of settlement negotiations may be in violation of the Model Code, DR 7–105(a) which provides: "A lawyer shall not present, participate in presenting or threaten to present criminal charges solely to obtain an advantage in a civil matter." In the case of *In re Charles* (1980), for example, a lawyer who participated in threatening to bring criminal charges during the course of settlement negotiations was held to have violated DR 7–105(a) even though the charges were never brought and the settlement was never consumated.

VI. LEGAL ASPECTS OF NEGOTIATION

A. THE SETTLEMENT AGREEMENT

1. Policy Favoring Settlement

The general policy of the law favors compromise and settlement for the obvious benefits which settlement brings—less litigation and thus less cost in terms of time and money for the parties and the courts. When there is a legal challenge to the validity of a settlement agreement, the courts will usually articulate a general legal policy favoring compromise and enforce the disputed agreement. Encouraging settlement however, is a legal policy, not an absolute goal, and the courts will overturn

settlement agreements which fail to meet the basic
requirements of contract law. In negotiating a
settlement agreement therefore, it is important to
keep in mind general contract law principles regarding the validity and enforcement of contracts.

(i) The Agreement

Settlement agreements are created, like other
contracts, with a valid offer and acceptance. General contract principles apply here with respect to
the requirements of an offer and the time within
which it may be accepted. While as a general rule,
settlement agreements need not be in writing, local
court rules or the statute of frauds may require a
writing.

(ii) Consideration

The general rules of contract apply to consideration in settlement agreements. By compromising a
disputed claim, an aggrieved party gives up the
right to litigate and at the same time avoids the
transaction costs of going to court, i.e., expense,
delay and uncertainty of court outcome. If the
disputed claim turns out to be invalid, the settlement agreement will still be upheld as long as the
party giving up the claim reasonably believes in its
validity.

(iii) Legality

Despite the policy of the law favoring settlement agreements, disputing parties do not forfeit their contract rights when they enter into settlement agreements. Like all other contracts, settlement agreements may be challenged on the grounds of fraud, duress, illegality, misrepresentation, lack of capacity, mistake, undue influence, and as violative of public policy.

It is important to pay attention to the relevant statute of limitations during settlement discussions. If negotiations continue until the statute of limitations runs out, the other disputing party has a potential defense to an action. For, unless a potential defendant has engaged in wrongful conduct, courts hold that continuing settlement negotiations do not prevent the statute of limitations from running.

2. Validity of Settlement Agreements

(i) In General

General contract principles apply to the validity of settlement agreements. Even though courts usually adopt a policy of favoring settlement agreements, if traditional contract defenses such as fraud, duress, undue influence, illegality and lack of capacity are established, the agreement may be set aside.

(ii) Guaranteed Verdict Agreements

Courts also set aside settlement agreements where public policy interests are implicated. One such area concerns contribution issues with joint tortfeasors and "Mary Carter" or "guaranteed verdict" agreements which guarantee that the plaintiff will obtain a minimum recovery and establish a ceiling on the settling defendant's liability. Mary Carter agreements, the name of which derives from the case of *J.D. Booth v. Mary Carter Paint Company* (1967), operate generally as follows: one or more defendants agrees to settle with the plaintiff for a specific amount of money. If the plaintiff recovers more than this amount from the non-settling defendants in a subsequent court action, the liability of the defendants who settled is reduced by that amount.

Mary Carter agreements have received mixed reviews from the legal community. Despite their popularity with defendants in complex tort litigation, legal scholars have criticized them because of the potential prejudice to non-settling defendants. Several states have held them void on public policy grounds, as constituting maintenance and champerty (supporting or promoting another person's litigation) as well as being violative of the cannons of ethics.

3. Court Approval of Settlement Agreements

Even though negotiation is essentially a private activity, there are some situations which require court approval before a settlement agreement becomes binding on the parties. Settlement agreements in class action litigation or involving minors are classic examples. In determining whether to approve such a proposed agreement, a trial court must analyze the facts and law relevant to the proposed compromise. The court must focus its inquiry on the actual terms of the settlement and compare them with the likely rewards the class or minor would have received following a successful trial of the case. Approval will be granted if the court finds that the settlement is fair, reasonable and is not the result of collusion. The court must document this conclusion in the record so that an appellate court will have a basis for review.

Other examples of agreements requiring judicial approval include divorce settlements, agreements by fiduciaries for the benefit of their wards, agreements where the public interest may be implicated such as antitrust, patent or trademark cases and, of course, criminal plea bargains.

B. PROTECTING CONFIDENTIALITY IN NEGOTIATION

Good lawyering demands careful consideration of what to disclose in a settlement negotiation. No lawyer wants to expose her client to the possibility of having admissions of liability introduced at a future trial if the negotiation breaks down. Confidentiality is, therefore, an essential ingredient in the negotiation process and the rules of evidence play an important role in protecting it.

Under the common law, an offer to compromise a disputed claim is inadmissible in a later trial to prove the validity or amount of the claim on the theory that the offer has little probative value. Rather than being construed as an admission of liability, the offer is viewed as an effort to avoid the transaction costs associated with litigation. It is therefore excluded from a later trial because of the public policy favoring the compromise of claims. Factual statements made during compromise negotiations may be admissible in a later trial, however, unless such statements are made in hypothetical terms or are prefaced with such phrases as "without prejudice," or "for purposes of discussion only."

Federal Rule of Evidence 408 (Appendix) expands the common law evidentiary exclusionary rule to include not only offers of compromise but also "evidence of conduct or statements made in compromise negotiations," thereby avoiding the distinctions between hypothetical and factual statements. Like the common law rule, Federal Rule 408 is limited to situations where evidence is introduced at trial to prove the validity or amount of the claim. Rule 408 does not allow exclusion if the evidence is offered for other purposes such as proving bias or prejudice, undue delay or obstruction of justice. A majority of states have adopted some version of Federal Rule 408.

While Rule 408 and its state counterparts give broad protection when the issue is admissibility, it does not necessarily protect information from discovery. The Federal Rules of Civil Procedure provide for a very liberal range of discovery. Rule 26(b) provides generally that parties "may obtain discovery regarding any matter not privileged, which is relevant to the subject matter involved in the pending action." Relevance in the context of discovery is broader than that required for admissibility at trial.

C. INCENTIVES FOR SETTLEMENT

1. Judicial Settlement Conferences

Judicial activism in settling lawsuits has received increasing attention in recent years. Rule 16 of the Federal Rules of Civil Procedure (Appendix) and its state counterparts, is a powerful tool for judges to hold pre-trial conferences and gain early control over litigation. In complex cases, judges may assign magistrates to conduct pre-trial conferences.

Many lawyers believe that judicial involvement enhances the settlement process. Instead of having to decide whether to be the first to initiate settlement discussions and risk appearing to have a weak case, the lawyer can rely on the judge to call the parties together for initial settlement talks. The judge, acting in a mediative capacity, offers a neutral perspective and gives the litigating parties a sense of where the case might be going. The negotiating lawyers bring this perspective back to their clients who may then be more inclined to accept a settlement offer.

There are some concerns, however, about the dangers of judicial coercion where parties are compelled to attend settlement conferences. In *G. Heileman Brewing Company, Inc. v. Joseph Oat Corporation* (1989) the Seventh Circuit Court of Appeals upheld the right of a federal magistrate to compel the Joseph Oat Corporation to send a "corporate representative with authority to settle" to a pretrial conference. The court relied on the Rules of Civil Procedure, particularly Rule 16, and the inherent power of a court to manage its docket. In a dissenting opinion Judge Posner expressed concerns about judicial coercion and wrote that "there are obvious dangers in too broad an interpretation of the federal courts inherent power to regulate their procedure. One danger is that it encourages judicial high-handedness ...."

2. Rule 68 FRCP

Rule 68 of the Federal Rules of Civil Procedure (Appendix) and its state counterparts, give the party who is defending a claim the opportunity to settle by making a formal offer of judgment. The party who rejects the settlement offer does so at her economic peril for she is liable for sanctions if she obtains a final judgment that is not "more favorable" than the settlement offer. In order to determine whether the final judgment is more or less favorable than the Rule 68 settlement offer, courts usually do a simply money calculation and compare the money amounts of the offer with the amount of the judgment. If the amount of final judgment is less than the settlement offer, the prevailing plaintiff is required to pay all "costs incurred after the making of the offer."

The purpose of Rule 68 is to encourage pretrial settlement and to avoid litigation. Although it has not been used frequently since its enactment in 1938, the Supreme Court's decision in *Marek v. Chesny* (1985) may change this especially with respect to civil rights litigation. *Marek* arose under 42 U.S.C.A. § 1983 and involved a civil rights action against three police officers. In responding to a domestic violence call, the officers shot and killed plaintiff Chesny's son. Prior to trial, the officers made a timely Rule 68 settlement offer of $100,000 which specifically included costs and attorneys fees. The plaintiff rejected the offer and the case was tried before a jury which awarded him less than the Rule 68 offer. Subsequently, the plaintiff filed a request for costs and attorney's fees pursuant to the Civil Rights Attorney's Fees Awards Act of 1976, 42 U.S.C.A. § 1988, under which a prevailing party in a § 1983 action may be awarded attorney's fees as part of the costs. The police officers opposed the granting of any post-offer attorney's fees on the ground that these fees were part of the costs that plaintiff was required to pay as sanctions under Rule 68. The district court agreed with the police officers and refused to award the plaintiff costs, including attorney's fees, incurred after the offer of judgment. This decision was reversed by the Court of Appeals for the Seventh Circuit.

The Supreme Court held that the officers had made a valid offer of judgment under Rule 68 and that the term "costs" as used in Rule 68 included attorneys fees awarded under 42 U.S.C.A. § 1988. The Court rejected the assertion that subjecting civil rights plaintiffs to Rule 68 curtails their access to the courts or deters them from bringing lawsuits. Rather, Rule 68 would serve as a disincentive for the plaintiff's attorney to continue litigation after the defendant makes a settlement offer. The effect of the Court's interpretation of Rule 68 may significantly effect the economic aspects of civil rights litigation. Defense counsel who are dealing with plaintiffs suing under any of the fee shifting type of statutes, might find Rule 68 an attractive option in generating an early settlement.

NEGOTIATION BIBLIOGRAPHY

Bastress and Harbaugh, *Interviewing Counseling and Negotiating: Skills For Effective Representation* (1990);

David A. Binder, Paul Bergman and Susan C. Price, *Lawyers as Counselors* (1990);

David A. Binder and Susan C. Price, *Legal Interviewing and Counseling* (1977);

Wayne D. Brazil, *Effective Approaches to Settlement: A Handbook for Lawyers and Judges (1988);*

Roger Fisher and William Ury, *Getting to Yes* (1981);

Donald G. Gifford, *Legal Negotiation Theory and Applications* (1989);

David A. Lax and James K. Sebenius, *The Manager as Negotiator,* (New York 1986);

Roy J. Lewicki and Joseph A. Litterer, *Negotiation,* (Illinois 1985);

Menkel-Meadow, *"Toward Another View of Legal Negotiation: The Structure of Problem-Solving,"* 31 U.C.L.A.L.Rev. 754 (1984).

Howard Raiffa, *The Art and Science of Negotiation* (1982);

Thomas C. Schelling, *The Strategy of Conflict* (1980);

Larry L. Teply, *Legal Negotiation in a Nutshell* (1991).

William Ury, *Getting Past No: Negotiating With Difficult People* (1991).

Gerald Williams, *Legal Negotiation and Settlement* (1983).

CHAPTER 3
MEDIATION
I. OVERVIEW

Mediation is an extension of the negotiation process. Disputing parties who have been unable to settle use a neutral third party to assist them in reaching an agreement. Unlike the adjudication process where a third party applies law to the facts to reach a result, in mediation a third party assists the disputants in applying their values to the facts and reaching a result. These values may include: the law; a sense of fairness; religious preferences; morals; and ethical concerns. The distinguishing feature of mediation is that the disputing parties, rather than the third party neutral, choose the norms which will influence the result of their dispute.

The use of mediation to resolve disputes is not a new phenomenon in the United States. Early immigrant groups resorted to their own mediation models rather than embrace the American system of justice. For some of these groups, including the Quaker, Chinese and Jewish communities, their own mediation mechanisms operated to insulate them from a foreign legal culture.

Organized labor has used mediation since the passage of the Arbitration Act of 1888 which provided for mediation as well as arbitration of railway labor disputes. The Erdman Act of 1898 also provided for mediation of railway disputes and the Newlands Act of 1913 established an official dispute resolution mechanism to manage railway disputes—the Board of Mediation and Conciliation. Mediation continued to be used in labor disputes with the passage of the Railway Labor Act of 1926, which created the National Mediation Board and the Taft–Hartley Act (1947), which established the Federal Mediation and Conciliation Service. Title II of the Taft–Hartley Act reflects a strong Congressional policy favoring mediation:

It is the policy of the United States that ... the settlement of issues between employers and employees through collective bargaining may be advanced by making available full and adequate governmental facilities for conciliation, mediation, and voluntary arbitration to aid and encourage employers and representatives of their employees to reach and maintain agreements ...

Section 201(b) of Title II of the Taft Hartley Act.

Since the early 1970's, mediation has transcended religious, ethnic, and labor interests to become a method of processing a wide variety of disputes. It is now a common feature in the judicial system in small claims courts, housing courts, family courts, some criminal court programs and neighborhood justice centers. In a growing number of jurisdictions mediation has become a mandatory prerequisite to trial. Mediation is also used in private commercial and family law practice and in school and environmental disputes.

A. DEFINITION

Mediation is generally understood to be a short-term, structured, task-oriented, participatory intervention process. Disputing parties work with a neutral third party, the mediator, to reach a mutually acceptable agreement. Unlike the adjudication process, where a third party intervenor *imposes* a decision, no such compulsion exists in mediation. The mediator aids the parties in reaching a consensus. It is the parties themselves who shape their agreement.

The traditional ideal of mediation contemplates a voluntary, private setting with individual members of ethnic or religious groups. The disputants share common values and have relatively equal bargaining strength. This assumption is being challenged today with the growth of mandatory and court-annexed mediation programs. Empirical studies of some court-annexed mediation programs suggest that even where parties have no prior or continuing relationship or shared values, the mediation process may still be successful. More empirical study is needed, however, to identify the principles which underlie successful mediation in mandatory court-annexed programs.

The growth of non-traditional mediation programs today has led to further classification of mediation as either *rights-based* or *interest-based*. In a rights-based mediation process, the parties' decision-making is tempered by what they think would be available to them in court if the case were litigated. In this type of process, there is more focus on the immediate dispute rather than the underlying conflict. An exclusive emphasis on rights, however, encourages positional bargaining and undercuts the value of the mediation process. Interest-based mediation, on the other hand, is a somewhat more therapeutic process. It more closely resembles the traditional ideal of mediation which attempts to help disputing parties understand the underlying needs and interests of the other party. Here, there is much more focus on the underlying conflict which gave rise to the dispute.

B. ADVANTAGES AND DISADVANTAGES OF MEDIATION

1. Advantages

The mediation process is viewed as more expeditious, inexpensive, and procedurally simple than adversarial problem solving. It enables the parties to define what is satisfactory to them by transcending the narrow issues in the dispute to focus on the underlying circumstances that contributed to the conflict. What looks like an isolated harassment case may well be a long story about years of hostilities between the parties. In the mediation process the disputing parties are able to deal with these long-standing hostilities and vent their anger in ways that would not be possible in the adversarial process. The mediator can assist the parties in unveiling hidden agendas and emotional baggage unhampered by the rules of evidence and procedure.

Moreover, mediation helps the parties re-adjust their conflicting perspectives and view their concerns in a much broader framework than simply "legal" issues in a legal system. Disputing parties begin to see themselves and their opponents in a different light. As Professor Lon Fuller states in his classic essay on the central quality of mediation: mediation has the "capacity to reorient the parties toward each other, not by imposing rules on them, but by helping them to achieve a new and shared perception of their relationship, a perception that will direct their attention toward each other."

Finally, mediation has great potential as an empowering process. Disputing parties have considerably more autonomy in mediation than they would in an adjudication process where a judge or arbitrator would impose a decision. In mediation, the disputants control the outcome of the process and this usually results in a high degree of compliance with mediated agreements. Empirical studies of some court-annexed mediation programs show that parties have a greater commitment to abide by a mediated agreement than with a court judgment.

2. Disadvantages

Mediation as a process is independent of the judicial system and therefore lacks the procedural and constitutional protections of adversarial justice, such as the right to a jury trial and the right to counsel. The expected tradeoff is that mediation will result in an agreement which is more responsive to individual needs than a court judgment. The underlying assumption here is that the agreement reached will be a fair one.

Fairness, however, is not an easily identifiable outcome, particularly where third parties not present at the mediation sessions may be affected. For example, what may be an acceptable agreement to parents in a divorce mediation, may seem quite unfair to the children who will be affected by the agreement. Furthermore, if parties reach an agreement in mediation without knowing what is available to them from a legal perspective, there is a risk of unfairness in the agreement. Additionally, in those instances where one of the parties has greater bargaining power whether from sheer force of personality, knowledge of law, better grasp of the facts or emotional or economic power, the result may be unfair to the other party.

Looking beyond the issue of fairness to participants, it is important to understand that mediation is neither a "truth" nor a "fault" inquiry. The question of who is right and who is wrong is less important than the question of how the problem can be resolved or the future defined. Disputing parties who need a vindication of their rights or a determination of fault will probably be unsatisfied with the mediation process.

Finally, successful mediation depends upon the parties' willingness to come to the bargaining table in good faith. Good faith is a difficult requirement to enforce in any dispute resolution process including litigation. Some parties may be using the process as a fishing expedition or simply to stall the litigation process. The mediator must guard against these abuses and be prepared to suspend or terminate the process if necessary.

II. THE MEDIATION PROCESS

A. SPECIFIC ACTIVITIES

In the mediation process, a neutral third party assists the disputing parties with the goal of helping them to arrive at a fair agreement. The core activities in this process are the information exchange and bargaining and these activities may be carried out in joint meetings, in private sessions known as caucuses or both. The mediation process usually begins with all of the disputing parties telling their stories in face-to-face negotiations. After the initial discussion of each person's view of the situation, and depending upon the issues involved, the mediator may break-out into private caucus sessions.

Mediation works best when it is a private, confidential proceeding. Confidentiality helps the mediator to build trust and develop a constructive rapport with the parties. Confidentiality also makes it safe for the parties to give information. It creates a safe space where parties can share their needs and interests without fear of reprisals.

The number of stages in the mediation process has been variously identified by different writers. The nature of the process depends upon a host of variables ranging from subject matter and mediator style to whether legal or judicial review is required. But, there are specific activities associated with the mediation process which are constant; although mediation is usually depicted as a linear process, there is often a high degree of interaction between the various activities. The mediator's work may be described generally as follows:

1. screen case;
2. explain the process to the parties;
3. assist parties with information exchange and bargaining;
4. assist parties in defining and drafting the agreement.

1. Screening

Mediation is not a panacea for the ills of the adversary system and not every case is appropriate for this process. Before beginning any mediation the mediator should conduct two preliminary inquiries: a) Is this an issue which is properly the subject of mediation? b) Are these parties ready for this process?

Depending upon the setting, the initial screening assessment may or may not be conducted by the mediator. Some types of disputes, such as those related to the custody of children, are subjected to mediation by virtue of statutes or local court rules. Thus, the mediator may be encountering resistant parties for the first time at the mediation session itself. Screening is also affected by public policy questions related to the appropriateness of mediating cases involving domestic violence, antitrust violations and criminal matters. Additionally, in any situation where a precedent is desirable, mediation may not be appropriate.

The second inquiry focuses on the parties' disposition and the stage of the conflict. Are there power imbalances between the parties? Are these parties ready for the process of mediation or are they too hostile to negotiate? Are they too polarized or entrenched in their positions to negotiate in good faith? Mediation is less likely to be effective if a good faith desire to settle is missing.

2. Mediator Describes Process and Role of Mediator

Even though one or both of the parties may understand how mediation works, it is useful for the mediator to explain the process in the presence of both parties at the joint session. In this way all parties share the same information. This is typically accomplished in an opening statement by the mediator at the beginning of the first session.

[Sample] Contents for an opening statement:

(a) *Mediator's name and credentials.* e.g., "Good morning. My name is Mary Smith. I am an attorney and have practiced family law for five years. I have mediated several custody disputes over the last three years."

(b) *Neutrality and impartiality.* This is the time to tell the parties of any prior relationship you may have had with either of them or any bias you may have in connection with the dispute. e.g., "I have not met either one of you before this meeting today and I have no opinion on the merits of this dispute."

(c) *Explanation of the process.* e.g., "Mediation is a process where both of you have the opportunity and the power to decide how to resolve this dispute. I am here to help you do this. I am not here to tell you what to do or to impose an agreement upon you."

(d) *Mechanics.* e.g., "Each of you will have the opportunity to discuss how you view the situation and you should not interrupt each other. I may meet with each of you privately. These meetings are called caucuses and sometimes they are quite helpful in giving people a chance to express fully how they feel about a particular problem. You can decide how much of our discussion remains private. Whatever information you tell me not to repeat, I will keep confidential."

At this point the mediator may discuss other matters such as fees, number of helpful persons who may sit in on the sessions, number of sessions and scheduling, etc.

(e) *Confidentiality.* The parties may decide to agree about the extent to which their communications will be kept confidential. Otherwise, the mediator may discuss the limits of confidentiality within a particular jurisdiction, including relevant evidentiary exclusion rules and privilege statutes.

(f) *Mediation outcomes.* This will depend upon the law in individual jurisdictions. If an agreement is reached in mediation, it may be enforceable as a contract. In some court-annexed programs, the mediation agreement becomes a court judgement. If an agreement is not reached, however, the parties have the option of deciding whether or not to pursue their claim in another forum.

Dealing With Hostility

Before beginning to assist parties with the information exchange and bargaining, the mediator must be conscious of the parties' behavior towards each other. If there is a high level of hostility between the parties, it may be necessary for the mediator to be assertive about the groundrules in the beginning of the session so that the parties do not recreate the same behavior which led to the dispute. Mutual respect is the cornerstone rule. It is important to remember that throughout the process, the mediator models behavior for the disputing parties.

3. Mediator Assists Parties With Information Exchange and Bargaining

Tasks:

(a) Collecting pertinent information

(b) Framing the issues

(c) Isolating points of agreement and disagreement

(d) Generating options

(e) Encouraging compromise so as to bring closure

The information exchange begins when the mediator makes the initial contact with the parties and they begin to educate each other about the dynamics of the controversy. For instance, are there entrenched positions, long-standing hostilities, misperceptions, poor communication? Information is not just limited to the substantive and factual aspects of the dispute but includes the parties' feelings, attitudes and mindsets.

Disputing parties bring much baggage to mediation. There is, at one level, the dispute which brought them there, e.g., the custody battle, the breached contract, the unpaid rent. At another level, there is an emotional component. Often, parties may be confused, angry, or hurt when they believe that they have been wronged. Other parties may have the need for an apology. This emotional baggage may present the real stumbling blocks to a mediated settlement. Therefore, the mediator must be skilled at understanding and acknowledging these feelings and drawing out hidden agendas if the final agreement is to satisfy the parties' real needs and interests.

The initial information acquisition process is a necessary prelude to framing issues, isolating points of agreement and generating options for settlement. It is important to remember however, that mediation is not a linear, but, an on-going interactive process. Information is constantly being acquired and re-interpreted. Issues are framed and re-framed as information is offered and refined.

4. Mediator Assists Parties in Drafting Agreement

Mediation agreements may be oral or written and they will vary considerably depending upon the context. In court-annexed or mandatory mediation programs, the agreement may be written on a one page stipulation form, whereas in a custody or divorce case, the agreement may be quite lengthy and detailed. In assisting parties in drafting a mediation agreement, the focus should be on initially producing a "working draft." The mediator must be sure that the parties fully understand the content of their agreement and the consequences of failing to comply with it.

What may have seemed like a point of agreement during the parties' discussions can be lost when it is reduced to writing. Thus, the challenge in drafting is to prevent a new dispute from arising over the terms of the agreement.

The tone of the agreement should be positive and emphasize what the parties have agreed to do rather than what they will refrain from doing. Unless there is good reason to be deliberately vague, time limits should be included to give closure to the agreement. For example, "Amanda Jones agrees to pay Paul Jones $2000.00 for the back rent owed by June 1, 1992" is better than "Amanda Jones agrees to pay Paul Jones $2000.00." The latter statement is open-ended and may invite litigation at any time Paul Jones decides that he should have been paid.

The mediator might also consider whether the parties wish to include a clause that they will return to mediation if there is a breach of the agreement. Finally, depending upon the nature of the dispute, the mediator may advise the parties to have independent legal review of the agreement before signing it. The ABA Standards of Practice for Lawyer–Mediators in Family Disputes require that the lawyer-mediator advise the parties to do this.

B. ROLE OF THE MEDIATOR

Throughout all of these stages the mediator is the control person. The mediator interprets concerns, relays information between the parties, frames issues, and re-focuses the problems. How these functions are accomplished depends upon the mediator's personal style and the level of hostilities between the parties. In some cases, the mediator facilitates by giving the parties control of the agenda and walking them through a problem-solving process. Other conflict situations may require more intense intervention in the process and the mediator would make specific suggestions, deliberately control the agenda and limit conversation.

Silbey and Merry have constructed two types of mediation styles based on their study of mediation: the bargaining and the therapeutic style. The bargaining mode is a pragmatic approach to reaching a settlement with more emphasis on the parties' bottom line than on hidden feelings. The mediator assumes a directive style and leads the parties towards agreement. Silbey and Merry report some comments of mediators who adopt a bargaining mode:

(a) I get people talking, then focus on some issues to get to agreement points. You can't just keep talking.

(b) I take a ball of broad issues and expand it by breaking it down into concrete ones. I see what issues really matter to them and I work on those.

(c) As a mediator, your job is to convince one or the other party to give up something; to negotiate together. The essence of the process is negotiation. You don't accept blame from others of each other, and you also don't accept their version of the facts. I am firm with a loudmouth. In small claims cases, I say that when a person won't settle, I will give it back to the judge and the judge will give him only 30 days to pay.

A therapeutic strategy emphasizes the emotional content of disputes and focuses on the communicative aspects of the mediation process. Disputing parties are taught the value of resolving conflict through peaceful discourse and are encouraged to fully express their feelings. The following comments illustrate the strategy of mediators who adopt a therapeutic strategy:

(a) My strategy is to try to get the recalcitrant person to see the other's view. If the other person doesn't do it, I do it in caucus myself. It usually works to point out how the other person sees things—that usually produces an agreement.

(b) I look for people's concerns, the reasons why this is important to each of them, and try to create an environment where they feel safe enough to articulate that concern. I do this by being open and non-judgmental and by listening to their feelings.

(c) I try just to get people talking, to get them to explain their side fully so that the other side really understands them. The problem is that people don't understand each other's thinking. I try to help them look for solutions.

As these varied mediator comments illustrate, there is no one "correct" way to mediate. Whether a mediator adopts a bargaining or therapeutic style or a variation of these, depends upon the mediator's own comfort level with each approach, the nature of the issues involved and the personalities of the disputing parties. Mediating a commercial dispute between two business persons with an on-going relationship may well call for a different approach than mediating a disputed child custody case with hostile parents.

C. MEDIATOR SKILLS

There is no magic formula which guarantees a successful mediation. Certainly, a mediator must be tolerant, patient, resourceful and articulate. In connecting mediation practice to a theory of lawyering, other skills of a good mediator are quite similar to those of the lawyer in listening, questioning, observing, interviewing, counseling, negotiating.

1. Listening

In developing the skill of listening, it is important to distinguish between the factual and substantive aspects of a dispute and the emotional feelings which react to those facts. The mediator who is really listening will hear the facts as well as understand the emotions attached to them.

Listening skills are essential. The mediator listens to acquire information and model behavior for the disputing parties. Often, lawyers have a difficult time practicing the art of listening. They may be thinking of the next question while their client is talking or wondering whether their client is telling the truth or trying to make the facts fit a specific cause of action. The lawyer who acts as a mediator must overcome this occupational handicap and temporarily suspend the "lawyering" mindset.

It is important that all of the parties perceive that they are being heard. It may well be that, ultimately, a particular dispute is not resolved according to a person's original expectations. However, if the disputant believes that someone has really listened to her, she will likely be satisfied. This is particularly true in some forms of court-annexed mediation where parties may simply want their day in court. In these instances, they do not necessarily need or desire black-robed justice but simply a neutral third party to listen with understanding to their grievances.

Developing good listening skills is not just an intuitive process. The mediator must concentrate on understanding what has been said and relaying this understanding back to the parties. The mediator uses active listening techniques such as rephrasing or reflecting for the parties what she has heard to make sure that she understands them. Good listening is not simply repeating what you heard.

Example 1

The husband in a custody dispute tells the mediator: "My wife is such a selfish person. She cares only about her patients and nothing else. If her own kids were sick, she would still be off to the hospital to care for her patients. That's just the type of driven nut that she is. I can't imagine her giving any time to the kids if they were really in trouble and any judge that would grant her custody would have to be deranged."

Mediator Response

"You seem to have real concerns about how your children would be cared for if your wife were given custody considering how much time she spends with her work. It seems that your wife is very committed to her responsibilities at the hospital."

Comment: The mediator's response in this case focuses on the husband's real concern, the children, and deflects attention away from the husband's image of the wife as an evil person. Instead of labeling the wife as a workaholic or repeating the husband comment that she is a "driven nut," the mediator in more positive language says that she is "very committed to her responsibilities at the hospital." This response may help the husband to see his wife in a new light and re-focus his energy and concerns on the children.

Example 2

The landlord in a housing dispute tells the mediator: "I want this bum out right away. He was late with his rent this month and I don't want this kind of trouble. The apartment looks like a cyclone hit it. It's a royal mess. Everything is broken. You know, these people are all the same. They have no sense of cleanliness or respect for property."

Mediator response

"It sounds to me like you are worried about future non-payment of rent. You think that since your tenant was late this month, that he will probably continue to pay his rent late. You also seem to be concerned with how the apartment is being kept up and whether you will have to make expensive repairs."

Comment: The mediator acknowledges the landlord's anxious feelings instead of reminding him that the tenant is a "bum." The mediator's response also focuses the issue on the landlord's concern that this tenant's non-payment of rent may set a precedent with the other tenants. By rephrasing the landlord's comments in nonjudgmental language which acknowledges the real fear, i.e., future non-payment of rent, the mediator establishes a good setting for a trust relationship with the landlord.

2. Questioning

Information is also acquired by questioning, a process which should always reinforce the mediator's neutrality. A good way to begin is to use open-ended questions. "Ms. Jones, can you tell us how you see the situation that brings you to mediation?" When Ms. Jones finishes her story, the mediator will turn to Ms. Smith and ask an equally open-ended question. "Ms. Smith, can you tell us how you view the situation?" As the mediation session progresses and additional information is acquired, questioning should remain nonjudgmental.

Lawyers with their adversarial training tend to be overly technical when questioning and often engage in cross-examination style questions. A lawyer in the hypothetical disputed custody case in the first listening example might be inclined to say to the wife: "Isn't it a fact that you work very long hours at the hospital?" Obviously, this approach limits the possibility of developing any kind of constructive rapport with the wife. Compare the lawyer's question to the mediator's: "Dr. Smith, could you describe a typical work day at the hospital beginning with the time you arrive until the time you leave for home?" The mediator's nonthreatening, non-judgmental question will probably elicit more information than the lawyer's adversarial one.

Folberg and Taylor have identified two specific questioning skills, reflection and clarification, which are also useful to mediators in acquiring information throughout the process.

The mediator *reflects* when trying to understand or interpret unacknowledged feelings or when suggesting to a person the missing meaning behind his or her words. For example, the mediator might say to a parent in a custody dispute: "It is not uncommon for the parent who agrees to give up custody to feel depressed and a little guilty. Do you feel this way now?" This type of reflecting statement can reduce tension and increase rapport with that parent. When people know that you understand what they are trying to say, they are more comfortable in opening up.

Clarification confirms what has been said and eliminates conflicting information. The mediator gives the parties a more definite sense of where they are going. For example, in a landlord-tenant dispute, a mediator might say to the landlord: "A while ago you said that you would be willing to accept a payment schedule for prior rent due and work out an agreement regarding repairs. Can we move forward with that understanding?"

3. Observation

The mediator also acquires information by observing what the parties do and how they act in the presence of each other as well as in a private caucus. When do they become silent? When do they appear nervous, uneasy, restless? The mediator must interpret non-verbal communications such as body language and eye contact. Is one party's refusal to look at the other party a sign of nervousness or is it hostility? In observing the parties, it is important to be aware of possible cultural differences. The fact that a person never makes eye contact with the mediator or the other party may be a sign of respect in one culture and a sign of guilt in another.

D. REQUIREMENTS TO BE A MEDIATOR

The field of mediation is at a crossroads and it is not clear what skills and knowledge base are essential. Although efforts are underway to identify the requirements, mediators are not currently compelled to comply with any uniform standards for education, training or practice. Some states have dealt with this issue by statute, specifying so many hours of training or the subjects which must be studied in such training. For example, a Massachusetts statute provides:

... For the purposes of this section a "mediator" shall mean a person not a party to a dispute who enters into a written agreement with the parties to assist them in resolving their disputes and has completed at least thirty hours of training in mediation and who either has four years of professional experience as a mediator or is accountable to a dispute resolution organization which has been in existence for at least three years or one who has been appointed to mediate by a judicial or governmental body. M.G.L.A. ch. 233, § 23C.

The Society of Professionals in Dispute Resolution (SPIDR) created a commission to study the qualifications of mediators and arbitrators. One of the main principles recognized by the commission is that performance rather than paper credentials should be the central qualification criteria. The SPIDR commission has identified the following skills as necessary for competent performance as a mediator:

(a) ability to understand the negotiating process and the role of advocacy;

(b) ability to earn trust and maintain acceptability;

(c) ability to convert parties' positions into needs and interests;

(d) ability to screen out non-mediable issues;

(e) ability to help parties to invent creative options;

(f) ability to help the parties identify principles and criteria that will guide their decision making;

(g) ability to help parties assess their nonsettlement alternatives;

(h) ability to help the parties make their own informed choices;

(i) ability to help parties assess whether their agreement can be implemented.

National Institute of Dispute Resolution (NIDR) *Dispute Resolution Forum* 9 May 1989.

III. ETHICAL CONCERNS

A. IN GENERAL

Concern with ethical behavior should permeate all areas of mediation practice if the integrity of the process is to be maintained. Mediators must be alert to the possibility of coercion, unfairness and bargaining imbalance between the parties. If these elements are present and appear harmful to either of the disputing parties, the mediator should stop the process. This is consistent with the directives given to mediators in the ABA Standards of Practice for Lawyer–Mediators in Family Disputes (Appendix). The ABA Standards direct mediators to suspend or terminate mediation whenever continuation of the process would harm one or more of the participants.

Beyond these general concerns, mandatory mediation programs raise particular ethical considerations. The Committee on Law and Public Policy of the Society of Professionals in Dispute Resolution (SPIDR) has addressed many of these concerns in an excellent report on mandatory participation in ADR programs. A summary of the SPIDR report is reprinted in the Appendix.

Ideally, mediation is a voluntary process that takes place in private and requires the good faith and meaningful participation of the parties. These characteristics may be diluted, however, as mediation becomes institutionalized within the judicial system. When disputing parties are told by the court that they *must* submit to mediation before they are entitled to a trial, coercion issues arise. Compulsion should never be incorporated into the process itself. The critical moment for consensus and consent is in the parties' final agreement. Whether or not a disputing party enters into the mediation process voluntarily, that party should always leave the process with a sense of ownership of the agreement which resulted from it.

B. SPECIFIC ETHICAL CONCERNS FOR THE LAWYER–MEDIATOR

1. Conflict of Interest

Several bar associations have issued formal and informal ethics opinions on the propriety of attorney-mediation practice. Most of the opinions have been related to the conflict of interest problems which arise with divorce mediation. Some opinions prescribe the conditions under which mediation by lawyers is permissible, others prohibit the practice. Given the wide range of opinion, attorneys should become familiar with the thinking and rules of their own state bar before beginning a mediation practice.

Overall, the bar association ethics opinions reflect the adversarial structure of the Model Code of Professional Responsibility which focuses upon the advocacy role of the attorney. Many of the earlier opinions refuse to countenance attorney-mediation practice because of the conflict of interest restrictions in the Model Code. Canon 5 of the Model Code, for example, provides that: "A lawyer should exercise independent professional judgment on behalf of a client." An ethical consideration in Canon 5 refers to mediation but offers little practical guidance to the attorney-mediator. EC 5–20 provides:

A lawyer is often asked to serve as an impartial arbitrator or mediator in matters which involve present or former clients. He may serve in either capacity if he first discloses such present or former relationships. After a lawyer has undertaken to act as an impartial arbitrator or mediator, he should not thereafter represent in the dispute any of the parties involved.

In 1983 the ABA approved the Model Rules of Professional Conduct and recognized an "intermediary" role for lawyers. Rule 2.2 provides:

(a) A lawyer may act as intermediary between clients if:

(1) the lawyer consults with each client concerning the implications of the common representation, including the advantages and risks involved and the effect on the attorney-client privileges, and obtains each client's consent to the common representation;

(2) the lawyer reasonably believes that the matter can be resolved on terms compatible

with the clients' best interests, that each client will be able to make adequately informed decisions in the matter, and that there is little risk of material prejudice to the interests of any of the clients if the contemplated resolution is unsuccessful; and

(3) the lawyer reasonably believes that the common representation can be undertaken impartially and without improper effect on other responsibilities the lawyer has to any of the clients.

(b) While acting as intermediary, the lawyer shall consult with each client concerning the decisions to be made and the considerations relevant to making them, so that each client can make adequately informed decisions.

(c) A lawyer shall withdraw as intermediary if any of the clients so requests, or if any of the conditions stated in paragraph (a) is no longer satisfied. Upon withdrawal, the lawyer shall not continue to represent any of the clients in the matter that was the subject of the intermediation.

Commentators disagree about whether the substantive provisions of Rule 2.2 should apply to mediation particularly because the rule equates "common representation" with "intermediation." The first Comment to the rule limits its application to situations where a lawyer is representing two or more parties with potentially conflicting interests.

The second Comment further clarifies the scope of Rule 2.2. Comment 2 provides:

> The Rule does not apply to a lawyer acting as arbitrator or mediator between or among parties who are not clients of the lawyer, even where the lawyer has been appointed with the concurrence of the parties. In performing such a role the lawyer may be subject to applicable codes of ethics, such as the Code of Ethics for Arbitration in Commercial Disputes prepared by a joint Committee of the American Bar Association and the American Arbitration Association.

Clearer professional guidance is given to lawyer-mediators in the Standards of Practice for Lawyer Mediators in Family Disputes approved by the American Bar Association in 1984 (Appendix). The standards define family mediation as "a process in which a lawyer helps family members resolve their disputes in an informative and consensual manner." This definition reinforces the role of the lawyer-mediator as a facilitator who aids disputing parties in reaching a fair agreement. The lawyer-mediator does not act in a representational capacity. If the parties need legal representation, they should seek independent legal counsel to advise them and to protect their individual interests. This is not the role of the lawyer-mediator. Throughout the ABA standards, the lawyer-mediator is told to advise the parties of the desirability of obtaining independent legal advice.

2. Advertising

In addition to conflict of interest inquiries, bar association ethics opinions have responded to lawyer-mediator concerns about the permissible limits of advertising. In general, written lawyer advertising is permissible unless it is deceptive or misleading. Although some bar associations have permitted lawyers to identify themselves as lawyers when advertising mediation services, there is no uniformity in this area. A potential lawyer-mediator should check the status of advertising in the relevant jurisdiction and, if necessary, request an advisory opinion from the bar association.

IV. MEDIATION AND THE LAW

A. THE ROLE OF LAW

Mediation often occurs in the shadow of the legal system. Rules and laws may impact on the kind of outcome which the parties consider. The primary concern of mediation, however, is not legal rights but shared interests and values; law is one among many choices of values. Legal rules exist simply as a reference point in the mediation process and are not dispositive of the outcome. They do, however, provide some indication of how the parties' positions would balance should they go to court.

For example, law is relevant to two disputing business persons, A and B, who know that A has the legal right to sue B for B's breach of contract in failing to deliver computers on time when time was of the essence in the contract. A lawsuit, however, cannot achieve the same result as mediation in this case. A lawsuit will result in a determination that B was either right or wrong but the inherently adversarial nature of the litigation process may impair any future business relationship between A and B. On the other hand, it is not the function of mediation to determine who is right and who is wrong. In the mediation process, A and B will both decide what they think is a fair resolution of the problem. Because they reach a mutually advantageous result, their business relationship has the possibility of continuing.

The role of law becomes increasingly more significant in court-annexed mediation programs where parties go to court in the first instance to seek a vindication of their legal rights. In jurisdictions where mediation is a mandatory prerequisite to trial, it is important that the parties have a basic understanding of the legal parameters of their case. While there is no guarantee of how a judge will rule in a particular case, there is usually a predictable range of possible outcomes. Disputing parties should not enter into mediation settlement agreements without some awareness of these outcomes. Otherwise, the danger is too great that legal rights are being relinquished without informed consent, that expediency rather than justice is the goal and that the resulting agreements are, therefore, unfair.

B.   LAWYERS AND MEDIATION

Lawyers may assume a wide variety of participatory roles in mediation.   Most Americans usually consult a lawyer before beginning a lawsuit and in the interviewing and counseling process, lawyers help clients choose between the available range of dispute resolution processes from negotiation to full scale litigation.   Lawyers, therefore, often help to decide whether a client should try mediation before or during litigation.

Some of the factors which should be considered in deciding whether to advise clients to choose mediation include: (a) the client's desire to settle, i.e., does the client really want to resolve the problem or just "get even;" (b) the nature of the relationship between the disputing parties, i.e., long-term, on-going or a one-shot deal; (c) the type of relief desired, i.e., whether a precedent is desirable; (d) the client's financial situation; (e) time considerations; (f) predictability of legal outcome; (g) the parties' positions; (h) desirability of a private settlement.

In addition to referring a client to mediation, an attorney may function in a traditional lawyering role and act as a negotiator for a client during the mediation session.   Some clients may feel more comfortable with this approach particularly in court-annexed mediation programs where they may be required to participate in mediation. There are considerable downsides however, in having the lawyer, rather than the client, participate in the mediation process. Typically, the client becomes a non-participatory fixture who defers to the attorney's sense of fairness. The client never directly experiences the benefits of mediation and the total experience becomes a rights-based process. This is similar to what happens in the adjudication process where the client is also essentially a non-participant and the lawyer tells the story. The story is constructed as a "cause of action" with the total focus on the client's "rights" and little or no understanding of the client's underlying needs and interests. Thus, to the extent possible, disputing parties themselves should become involved in working through the mediation process to fully appreciate the sense of empowerment that mediation brings.

Lawyers also have a role in reviewing a mediation agreement for a client. The ABA Standards of Practice for Lawyer–Mediators in Family Disputes contemplate that the parties will seek independent legal review during the mediation process. In performing the review function, assuming the agreement is otherwise fair, lawyers must be cautious about substituting their own judgment for their client's. What is unacceptable for the lawyer who judges the agreement through a legal prism, may be more than satisfactory to the client who feels that his needs have been satisfied.

The role of mediator or co-mediator is a relatively new role for lawyers. One of the chief benefits of choosing a lawyer as a mediator is the lawyer's ability to help the parties explore the legal as well as the non-legal consequences of conduct. Lawyers are better able to help the parties engage in reality testing about what is involved in the litigation process as well as to understand the likely range of legal outcomes.

Lawyers should be able to inform disputants of the relevant law and suggest possible court outcomes. This should be done in general informational terms so as to avoid giving legal advice. In this regard, the ABA Standards of Practice for Lawyer Mediators in Family Disputes distinguish between a mediator defining legal issues (permissible) and interpreting the law (impermissible):

> The mediator may define the legal issues, but shall not direct the decision of the mediation participants based upon the mediator's interpretation of the law as applied to the facts of the situation. ...

As noted earlier in the section on ethical concerns for the lawyer mediator, there is a great deal of uncertainty over the appropriate role for lawyers who mediate. Some bar association ethics opinions equate mediation with representation and flatly prohibit the practice of attorney mediation. Other ethics opinions permit lawyers to mediate under carefully prescribed circumstances.

One of the most enlightened opinions regarding the permissible extent of a lawyer's involvement in the mediation process has been issued by the Association of the Bar of the City of New York. While the opinion responds specifically to an inquiry about a non-profit divorce mediation program, it provides helpful parameters for lawyers who wish to become involved in mediation. The factual background of the opinion involved an organization with a staff of licensed mental health professionals which provided marital and family therapy. The organization proposed to offer "structured mediation" in marital cases, a process which involves a trained therapist working with separating or divorcing couples to help them resolve issues such as property division, child custody, visitation and support. Part of the inquiry concerned whether a lawyer could (a) become part of the mediating team, (b) give impartial legal advice to the parties, such as advice on the tax consequences of a separation or divorce agreement, or (c) draft a divorce or settlement agreement after the terms of such agreement have been approved by the parties. After a thorough and thoughtful examination of a lawyer's involvement in mediation the opinion provides the following guidelines:

> ... we have concluded that lawyers may participate in the divorce mediation procedure proposed in the inquiry here, only on the following conditions.
>
> To begin with, the lawyer may not participate in the divorce mediation process where it appears that the issues between the parties are of such complexity or difficulty that the parties

cannot prudently reach a resolution without the advice of separate and independent legal counsel.

If the lawyer is satisfied that the situation is one in which the parties can intelligently and prudently consent to mediation and the use of an impartial legal adviser, then the lawyer may undertake these roles provided the lawyer observes the following rules:

First, the lawyer must clearly and fully advise the parties of the limitations on his or her role and specifically, of the fact that the lawyer represents neither party and that accordingly, they should not look to the lawyer to protect their individual interests or to keep confidences from the other.

Second, the lawyer must fully and clearly explain the risks of proceeding without separate legal counsel and thereafter proceed only with the consent of the parties and only if the lawyer is satisfied that the parties understand the risks and understand the significance of the fact that the lawyer represents neither party.

Third, a lawyer may participate with mental health professionals in those aspects of mediation which do not require the exercise of professional legal judgment and involve the same kind of mediation activities permissible to lay mediators.

Fourth, lawyers may provide impartial legal advice and assist in reducing the parties' agreement to writing only where the lawyer fully explains all pertinent considerations and alternatives and the consequences to each party of choosing the resolution agreed upon.

Fifth, the lawyer may give legal advice only to both parties in the presence of each other.

Sixth, the lawyer must advise the parties of the advantages of seeking independent legal counsel before executing any agreement drafted by the lawyer.

Seventh, the lawyer may not represent either of the parties in any subsequent legal proceedings related to the divorce.

Ethics Opinion, Committee on Professional and Judicial Ethics, Association of the Bar of the City of New York, Inquiry Reference No. 80–23.

C. LEGAL ISSUES

1. Confidentiality

The mediation process works effectively when the disputing parties participate in good faith and are willing to share their real needs and interests with each other and the mediator. The parties may be reluctant to speak openly, however, for fear that their statements will come back to haunt them and the mediator in future litigation if the mediation session breaks down. Other parties may fear that their opponent is using the mediation process as a discovery fishing expedition. Some lawyers, therefore, are reluctant to encourage their clients to participate in the mediation process, particularly in the face of on-going litigation.

These concerns have resulted in a great deal of writing about the need for protecting confidentiality in the mediation process. Not all commentators agree, however, on the extent to which confidentiality should be honored. Is absolute confidentiality necessary to safeguard the integrity of the mediation process? Or, should confidentiality be honored on a more limited basis? In either case, what happens to the well-established principle of law which holds that the public is entitled to every person's evidence? There is no uniform approach in this area. In counseling clients about protecting the confidentiality of the mediation process, lawyers should consider at least three means of protection: the evidentiary exclusionary rules, privilege and contract.

(i) Evidentiary Exclusionary Rules

Under the common law, an offer to compromise a disputed claim is inadmissible in a later trial to prove the validity or amount of the claim on the theory that the offer has little probative value. Federal Rule of Evidence 408 (Appendix) expands the common law rule to include not only offers of compromise but also "evidence of conduct or statements made in compromise negotiations." These evidentiary exclusionary rules are discussed more fully in Chapter 2 on the negotiation process.

No court has specifically ruled that the mediation process should be considered a settlement negotiation for purposes of the common law evidentiary exclusionary rule or Federal Rule of Evidence 408. The closest analogy is an EEOC conciliation case, wherein the court ruled that evidence arising in the conciliation hearing "probably is inadmissible under Fed.R.Evid. 408." *U.S. Equal Employment Opportunity Com'n v. Air Line Pilots Ass'n, Intern.* (1980).

Mediation is an extension of the negotiation process and it makes eminent sense to consider it as a settlement negotiation for purposes of the evidentiary exclusionary rules. This is the view of most commentators and one state, Colorado, has so ruled by statute:

> ... Mediation proceedings shall be regarded as settlement negotiations, and no admission, representation, or statement made in mediation not otherwise discoverable or obtainable shall be admissible as evidence or subject to discovery. In addition, a mediator shall not be subject to process requiring the disclosure of any matter discussed during mediation proceedings." Colo. Rev.Stat. 13–22–307 (Supp.1991).

(ii) Privilege

A privilege may provide a greater degree of protection to communications made in the mediation process than is available with the evidentiary exclusionary rules. In deciding whether or not to recognize a privilege for communications made in the mediation process, courts should consider the fundamental conditions set out in Wigmore's formulation:

1. The communications must originate in a confidence that they will not be disclosed.

2. This element of confidentiality must be essential to the full and satisfactory maintenance of the relation between the parties.

3. The relationship must be one which in the opinion of the community ought to be sedulously fostered.

4. The injury that would inure to the relation by the disclosure of the communications must be greater than the benefit thereby gained for the correct disposal of the litigation.

Wigmore *Evidence in Trials at Common Law* § 2285 McNaughton Edition 1961.

Courts may also recognize a mediation privilege based on public policy considerations. For example, in *N.L.R.B. v. Joseph Macaluso, Inc.* (1980), a case involving unfair labor practices, the testimony of a labor mediator was critical in resolving a factual dispute. The court, however, recognized a mediator privilege and held that the National Labor Relations Board could revoke the subpoena of a mediator even though the mediator could have provided information which was crucial to the resolution of the dispute in that case. The operative statutes and regulations in *Macaluso*, gave strong support to a public policy of complete exclusion of mediator testimony in labor cases. Thus, the court held "that the complete exclusion of mediator testimony is necessary to the preservation of an effective system of labor mediation, and that labor mediation is essential to continued industrial stability, a public interest sufficiently great to outweigh the interest in obtaining every person's evidence."

Several state statutes also protect mediation confidentiality through some type of privilege. Under many of these statutes, information from a mediation session is both inadmissible at trial and also protected from discovery. There is little uniformity among the states and the statutes vary concerning the content of what is privileged and the conditions under which the privilege may be invoked. Two statutory examples illustrate the differing range of approaches. In New York, for mediations conducted in community dispute resolution programs, there is a broad privilege which applies to all communications made in the mediation session. The Judiciary Law, section 849–b(6) provides in relevant part:

> ... all memoranda, work products, or case files of a mediator are confidential and not subject to disclosure in any judicial or administrative proceeding. Any communication relating to the subject matter of the resolution made during the resolution process by any participant, media-

tor, or any other person present at the dispute resolution shall be a confidential communication.

On the other hand, a California statute takes a more limited approach and provides that a mediation privilege is applicable only if the parties agree in writing that the information will be privileged. The California Evidence Code, section 1152.5 (Supp.1991) provides in relevant part:

Mediation

(a) Subject to the conditions and exceptions provided in this section, when persons agree to conduct and participate in a mediation for the purpose of compromising, settling, or resolving a dispute:

(1) Evidence of anything said or of any admission made in the course of the mediation is not admissible in evidence, and disclosure of any such evidence shall not be compelled, in any civil action in which, pursuant to law, testimony can be compelled to be given.

(2) Unless the document otherwise provides, no document prepared for the purpose of, or in the course of, or pursuant to, the mediation, or copy thereof, is admissible in evidence, and disclosure of any such document shall not be compelled, in any civil action in which, pursuant to law, testimony can be compelled to be given.

(b) Subdivision (a) does not limit the admissibility of evidence if all persons who conducted or otherwise participated in the mediation consent to its disclosure.

(c) This section does not apply unless, before the mediation begins, the persons who agree to conduct and participate in the mediation execute an agreement in writing that sets out the text of subdivisions (a) and (b) and states that the persons agree that this section shall apply to the mediation ....

(iii) Contract

Whether or not a privilege exists, parties who participate in the mediation process may establish additional safeguards by entering into a written confidentiality agreement. Such a contract could be a simple release in which the parties agree not to subpoena the mediator or request production of any information related to the mediation. Alternatively, a more detailed contract could be executed between the parties and the mediator specifically providing what is and is not confidential, e.g. the fact that the agreement was reached, the terms of the agreement itself, any details relating to the actual mediation process.

The ABA Standards of Practice for Lawyer Mediators in Family Disputes (Appendix) adopts a contract approach. The standards provide that at the beginning of the mediation session, the parties should agree in writing not to require the mediator to disclose any statements made during the mediation. The mediator agrees that if subpoenaed, he or she will inform the parties immediately so that they have an opportunity to quash the subpoena.

A contract approach is also adopted in the Center for Public Resources' Model Procedures for the Mediation of Business Disputes (1991). The model procedures, which can be incorporated by reference into a business agreement as well as into a post-dispute submission agreement, provide in relevant part:

8. The entire process is confidential. The parties and the mediator will not disclose information regarding the process, including settlement terms, to third parties, unless the parties otherwise agree. The process shall be treated as a compromise negotiation for purposes of the Federal Rules of Evidence and state rules of evidence.

. . .

10. Unless all parties and the mediator otherwise agree in writing,

(a) the mediator will be disqualified as a witness, consultant or expert in any pending or future investigation, action or proceeding relating to the subject matter of the mediation (including any investigation, action or proceeding which involves persons not party to this mediation); and

(b) The mediator and any documents and information in the mediator's possession will not be subpoenaed in any such investigation, action or proceeding, and all parties will oppose any effort to have the mediator and documents subpoenaed.

Parties who seek the assistance of private ADR organizations to administer their mediation may be adopting a contract approach if they agree to abide by the rules of that organization. For example, the American Arbitration Association's Commercial Mediation Rules have specific regulations governing the confidentiality of the mediation session. Rules 11 and 12 provide as follows:

11. *Privacy.* Mediation sessions are private. The parties and their representatives may attend mediation sessions. Other persons may attend only with the permission of the parties and with the consent of the mediator.

12. *Confidentiality.* Confidential information disclosed to a mediator by the parties or by witnesses in the course of the mediation shall not be divulged by the mediator. All records, reports, or other documents received by a mediator while serving in that capacity shall be confidential. The mediator shall not be compelled to

divulge such records or to testify in regard to the mediation in any adversary proceeding or judicial forum.

The parties shall maintain the confidentiality of the mediation and shall not rely on, or introduce as evidence in any arbitral, judicial, or other proceeding:

(a) views expressed or suggestions made by another party with respect to a possible settlement of the dispute;

(b) admissions made by another party in the course of the mediation proceedings;

(c) proposals made or views expressed by the mediator; or

(d) the fact that another party had or had not indicated willingness to accept a proposal for settlement made by the mediator.

While the contract approach overcomes the gaps inherent in the evidentiary exclusionary rules, it has some downsides. First, confidentiality contracts would not be binding on non-parties to the agreement who might be able to obtain the desired information through discovery requests. One way to overcome this hurdle, if mediation occurs as part of on-going litigation, is to seek a protective order from the court under FRCP 26(c) or its state counterparts.

Second, it is unclear whether the courts will enforce a private confidentiality agreement arising out of the mediation process. If, for example, there is a claim that a mediation agreement resulted from fraud, duress or coercion, a court might examine evidence from the mediation session in order to determine whether the agreement should be enforced. Certainly, the existence of a confidentiality agreement in mediation should not shield illegal behavior.

Many commentators rely on a marriage counseling case, _Simrin v. Simrin_ (1965) for the proposition that courts will enforce a confidentiality agreement in mediation. In _Simrin,_ a rabbi acting as a marriage counselor, agreed to counsel a husband and wife only after they had expressly agreed that their communications to him would be confidential and that neither would call him as a witness in the event of a divorce. After the parties were divorced, the wife sought the rabbi's testimony in a custody action and he refused to testify based on the prior confidentiality agreement. Responding to the wife's claims that suppression of evidence was against public policy, the court noted that public policy also favors procedures designed to preserve marriages. Thus, the court ruled that the rabbi need not reveal his conversations with the parties.

Equally strong public policy arguments can be made in the case of mediation. As an extension of the negotiation process, mediation helps parties to resolve disputed claims. It can be argued therefore, that because public policy favors the settlement of disputed claims, and assuming they are otherwise legal, that confidentiality agreements arising out of the mediation process should be honored.

2. Enforceability

There are two questions raised with the issue of enforceability in mediation: (1) whether an agreement to mediate is enforceable and (2) whether an agreement reached in mediation is enforceable.

(i) Agreements to mediate

One way to encourage the use of mediation is to insert a clause in a contract which provides that the parties will attempt to resolve all disputes arising out of the contract through mediation before resorting to arbitration or litigation. This agreement acts as a type of guarantee that the reluctant mediation user will cooperate. An example of a simple clause would be:

Mediation: If a dispute arises related to this contract, we agree to use our best efforts to resolve the dispute through the mediation process. We will both select the mediator. The costs of mediation shall be shared equally by us.

The little case law which does exist concerning the enforceability of such clauses suggests that the courts will be inclined to uphold them. The case of *AMF Inc. v. Brunswick, Corp.* (1985), is instructive. *Brunswick* involved the enforceability of a non-binding ADR clause in a settlement agreement which required that disputes over advertising claims be submitted to an advisory third party for a non-binding opinion. The clause at issue read as follows:

Both parties agree to submit any controversy which they may have with respect to data based comparative superiority of any of their products over that of the other to such advisory third party for the rendition of an advisory opinion. Such opinion shall not be binding upon the parties, but shall be advisory only.

In holding that the agreement was enforceable, the court noted that "public policy favors support of alternatives to litigation when these alternatives serve the interests of the parties and of judicial administration." If a Brunswick approach is followed in mediation cases, this would certainly enhance the public credibility of the process.

(ii) Agreements Reached in Mediation

Generally, under current practice, the mediation agreement is considered to be a contract and is enforced under the general principles of contract law. There are few cases concerning the enforceability of agreements reached in mediation. Perhaps the paucity of case law is due to the high degree of compliance associated with mediation agreements.

It is important to note, however, that enforcement issues may be complicated by confidentiality provisions. If for example parties have entered into a contractual agreement regarding communications made during mediation, it may be difficult to introduce evidence from the mediation session to prove a valid agreement or conversely to set aside an agreement on the grounds of fraud, duress or undue influence.

In an effort to enhance the quality of mediation practice and also to protect parties in the process, some states have enacted statutes which change existing contract law regarding the enforcement of mediation agreements. In Minnesota, for example, a mediation agreement is not binding unless the parties state specifically that it *is* binding. Minn. Stat.Ann. § 572.35 provides:

(iii) Effect of Mediated Settlement Agreement

The effect of a mediated settlement agreement shall be determined under principles of law applicable to contract. A mediated settlement agreement is not binding unless it contains a provision stating that it is binding and a provision stating substantially that the parties were advised in writing that (a) the mediator has no duty to protect their interests or provide them with information about their legal rights; (b) signing a mediated settlement agreement may adversely affect their legal rights; and (c) they should consult an attorney before signing a mediated settlement agreement if they are uncertain of their rights.

Some practitioners and writers have questioned the wisdom of applying contract law to the enforceability of mediation agreements. Under this view the real goal of mediation is the preservation of relationships and thus, it is not so much the agreement that is important as the understanding produced in the process of reaching that agreement. The notion of attaching legal consequences to the non-performance of the mediation agreement may destroy any potential for bringing parties to an agreement.

3. Liability of Mediators

Outside the labor field, organized mediation practice is a relatively recent phenomena. Therefore, it is not surprising that there is very little case law on mediator liability. Commentators have advanced a number of theories under which a mediator could be held liable by the parties. These include negligence, contract, invasion of privacy, defamation, and tortious interference with contractual relationship. As a practical matter, tort and contract will be the most feasible theories of liability.

(i) *Tort Liability Based in Negligence*

One of the obstacles to imposing tort liability on mediators is that it is difficult to pinpoint the duties which mediators owe to participants or third parties. Traditional negligence theory is predicated on the existence of a duty, breach of that duty, causation and damages. Mediators work in many different contexts and therefore, their duties may vary. Some indication of the minimal duties owed by a mediator is found in professional standards such as The Ethical Standards of Professional Responsibility of the Society of Professionals in Dispute Resolution (SPIDR) and the ABA Standards for Lawyer Mediators in Family Disputes, both of which are reprinted in the Appendix. The ABA Standards, the only specific guides given to attorney mediators, refer to six distinct duties: define and describe the process of mediation and its cost before the parties reach an agreement to mediate; protect information learned in the mediation process; be impartial; assure that the mediation participants make decisions based upon sufficient information and knowledge; suspend or terminate mediation whenever continuation of the process would harm one or more of the participants; advise each of the participants to obtain legal review prior to reaching any agreement. A violation of these standards is very good evidence of breach but it is not dispositive. Thus, the jury in a negligence action has limited legal authority for determining whether the defendant mediator breached a duty to the plaintiff.

Even where the plaintiff is able to show that the mediator owed and breached a duty, there is the additional difficulty of satisfying the causation requirement. The case of *Lange v. Marshall* (1981), is instructive. In *Lange,* an appellate court reversed a $74,000 jury verdict against a lawyer-mediator on the grounds that the plaintiff failed to prove that he caused her injury. The plaintiff argued that in attempting to assist her and her husband terminate their twenty-five year old marriage, the lawyer-mediator breached several duties. Specifically, he failed to (1) inquire as to the financial state of her husband and advise her accordingly; (2) negotiate for a better settlement; (3) advise her that she would obtain a better settlement if she litigated the matter; and (4) fully and fairly disclose to her the extent of her rights as to marital property, custody and maintenance. The plaintiff's causation argument was that, but for the lawyer-mediator's actions, her husband would have agreed to a more favorable divorce settlement. The *Lange* court found this argument highly speculative, stating that the causal connection between the mediator's conduct and the harm asserted was merely conjectural. Such weak evidence of causation, the court concluded, provided insufficient grounds for recovery, even if the defendant mediator had acted negligently.

(ii) Liability Issues in the Caucus

Use of the caucus raises some complicated issues related to confidentiality and mediator liability. Typically, in a caucus, the mediator will ask the parties to specify what information should be kept confidential. The mediator then assures the party that she will not disclose that information. Suppose the mediator learns in a caucus that child abuse has occurred in a family. Should that information remain confidential? In some states information related to child abuse is not considered confidential. Absent such a policy, however, the question arises as to what, if any, duty the mediator has to inform the proper authorities? Moreover, if the mediator learns information in a caucus that serious bodily harm will occur to the other party, the issue arises as to whether there is a duty to warn despite the prior assurances of confidentiality.

As outlined above, for a mediator to be found liable on a theory of negligence, she must owe a duty to the plaintiff. In the usual case the plaintiff will have been a party in the mediation process. But what about third parties who are not present at the mediation? Whether a mediator may also owe a duty to these individuals has been the subject of some debate.

As an example of a third-party scenario, suppose that two disputing parties in a commercial mediation case request that the mediator keep all information from the session confidential. The mediator agrees and then learns in a private caucus that one of the parties intends to inflict serious physical harm on her competitor, a third party. Does the mediator have a duty to inform the competitor of what she heard despite the earlier assurances of confidentiality?

Some commentators have looked to a California case, *Tarasoff v. Regents of the University of California* (1976), to support a theory of mediator liability in this type of case. In *Tarasoff,* a psychotherapist was found to be negligent for failing to warn a young woman of his patient's threats to murder her. According to the California Supreme Court, the doctor had a duty to disclose the threats because of the special relationship existing between doctor and patient. This special relationship, the *Tarasoff* court posited, required the psychotherapist to control his patient's conduct.

It is questionable whether the duty to disclose set out in *Tarasoff* should apply across the board in the mediation context. Professor Arthur Chaykin maintains that if *Tarasoff* is applicable in mediation, then the mediator would have to stand in a special relationship to the person threatened by a mediation participant. Usually, mediators lack the degree of control over participants needed to make the mediator-participants' relationship a special relationship engendering the *Tarasoff* duty to disclose. Another factor weighing against a mediator's duty to disclose might be that mediators who are not trained in psychology or psychiatry would lack the necessary expertise to determine whether threats of harm are real.

(iii) Contract Liability

It is becoming common for mediators to use written employment contracts in their practice.

This is a wise practice because a contract clarifies the extent of the mediators responsibilities and gives the parties a clear understanding of what is and is not promised. This is particularly important in the case of lawyer-mediators where parties' expectations for the mediator's performance may go beyond the bounds of appropriate mediator activity. For example, the lawyer-mediator may want to make sure that the parties understand that legal representation is not part of the mediation process or that specific legal advice will not be given to either party. This type of contract would have protected the attorney in a *Lange v. Marshall* situation where one of the parties later claims that the attorney mediator failed to represent her interests.

In addition to providing a measure of protection for the parties and the mediator, contracts can also serve as a basis of liability against the mediator. Thus, lawyers should be cautious in drafting mediation contracts and consider including such items as time limits for the mediation and specific demands on the mediator's performance. In some cases it may even be appropriate to include an exculpatory clause in the contract.

(iv) Immunity

Several states have enacted statutes which grant some type of civil immunity to mediators. The nature and extent of the immunities varies depending upon subject matter, e.g. farm debt, medical malpractice, or what type of program is involved, e.g. court-annexed mediation. Immunity may also be limited to certain types of behavior, such as reckless or wanton misconduct.

Absent a statute, mediators in a growing number of court-annexed programs may be protected under some species of judicial immunity. Court-annexed mediation programs share many of the characteristics of judicial settlement conferences. The mediator is a neutral third party appointed by the court who tries to assist litigants in arriving at a settlement. Common law judicial immunity has been extended to persons who are appointed by the court to perform a wide range of tasks within the judicial system and therefore, it may well apply to court-appointed mediators.

4. The Unauthorized Practice of Law Restrictions

The unauthorized practice of law doctrine restricts the practice of law to licensed attorneys who have satisfied specific educational requirements and have demonstrated good moral character. Canon 3 of the Model Code states that "a lawyer should assist in preventing the unauthorized practice of law" and the Model Rules prohibit lawyers from assisting any person who "is not a member of the Bar in the performance of activity that constitutes the practice of law." (Model Rule 5.5(b)). While this doctrine has come under attack in recent years as an attempt by the legal profession to preserve its professional monopoly, every jurisdiction still has laws which prohibit, with a few exceptions, non-lawyers from the practice of law.

Some confusion exists over whether the unauthorized practice of law doctrine applies to mediators, the majority of whom are non-lawyers. The concern here is that mediation may constitute the practice of law. This issue has arisen most frequently within the context of divorce mediation and several bar association ethics committees have issued opinions on the permissible boundaries of divorce mediation for lawyers and non-lawyers. Some typical inquiries in the opinions concern whether mediation constitutes the practice of law, the extent to which non-lawyers may participate in the mediation process, and the extent to which lawyers may participate in mediation with non-lawyers on their own.

Concern with unauthorized practice pervades the opinions but no coherent doctrine has emerged. Certainly, the mediation process itself is not the practice of law. And, it does not become so simply because it involves the resolution of legal issues. The prudent course of action for non-lawyer mediators, however, is to refer all requests for legal advice to the parties' attorneys. If the parties are not represented by counsel, the non-lawyer mediator should recommend that the parties seek the advice of an attorney before signing any final agreement which implicates their legal rights.

V. MEDIATION APPROACHES
IN A LITIGATED CASE:
ONE EXAMPLE

Until recently, the adversarial mindset has prevailed in the practice of law. In counseling clients with disputes, most lawyers have assumed that litigation was the norm and have had little encouragement to advise a client to try the mediation process. Court reporters are filled with cases which might have been settled through mediation with better results than those produced by litigation.

An example of a case which might have been a possible candidate for mediation is *Foster v. Preston Mill Co.* (1954). It is unclear from the reported facts whether mediation was attempted in this case. The facts are relatively straightforward. Blasting operations conducted by Preston Mill Company (defendant), frightened mother mink owned by B.W. Foster, (plaintiff) and caused the mink to kill their kittens. Foster sued his neighbor, Preston Mill to recover damages. The case was tried on a theory of absolute liability and in the alternative, a nuisance theory. Following a non-jury trial, the court rendered a judgment for Foster in the amount of $1953.68 on the theory that after Preston received notice of the effect which its blasting operations were having upon the mink, it was absolutely liable for all damages of that nature thereafter sustained. Preston Mill Company appealed this decision.

On appeal, the Supreme Court of Washington reversed the judgment of the trial court and held that the doctrine of absolute liability was inapplicable under the facts of the case.

Resolving this case through the adjudication process required that the court apply "law" to the "facts" and arrive at a conclusion. Excerpted below are a few passages which illustrate this process.

The primary question presented by appellant's assignments of error is whether, on these facts, the judgment against appellant is sustainable on the theory of absolute liability.

The modern doctrine of strict liability for dangerous substances and activities stems from Justice Blackburn's decision in Rylands v. Fletcher ... As applied to blasting operations, the doctrine has quite uniformly been held to establish liability, irrespective of negligence, for property damage sustained as a result of casting rocks or other debris on adjoining or neighboring premises. ...

There is a division of judicial opinion as to whether the doctrine of absolute liability should apply where the damage from blasting is caused, not by the casting of rocks and debris, but by concussion, vibration, or jarring .... This court has adopted the view that the doctrine applies in such cases ....

However the authorities may be divided on the point just discussed, they appear to be agreed that strict liability should be confined to consequences which lie within the extraordinary risk whose existence calls for such responsibility ....

This restriction which has been placed upon the application of the doctrine of absolute liability is based upon considerations of policy ....

Applying this principle to the case before us, the question comes down to this: Is the risk that any unusual vibration or noise may cause wild animals, which are being raised for commercial purposes, to kill their young, one of the things which make the activity of blasting ultrahazardous?

We have found nothing in the decisional law which would support an affirmative answer to this question. The decided cases, as well as common experience, indicate that the thing which makes blasting ultrahazardous is the risk that property or persons may be damaged or injured by coming into direct contact with flying debris, or by being directly affected by vibrations of the earth or concussions of the air ....

It is the exceedingly nervous disposition of mink, rather than the normal risks inherent in blasting operations, which therefore must, as a matter of sound policy, bear the responsibility for the loss here sustained.

Obviously, if the parties' goal was to obtain a precedent on the issue of absolute liability, then litigation was the proper choice of process. But consider the litigation "results" here. Three years passed before this dispute was resolved by the court. The case was tried, appealed, and decided again, with all the attendant financial, emotional, and temporal costs associated with litigation. The result was a "winner" and a "loser." Preston won a victory of sorts but at the cost of "saving" less than $2000.00. There were the transaction costs of legal fees, and time lost in testifying, etc. The mink farmer lost the income from thirty to forty kittens and remained uncompensated despite his foray into court.

A. SOME INDICATIONS FOR MEDIATION

(a) *Parties Desire to Settle:* The facts certainly show an initial willingness to compromise. When Preston told Foster about the damage to his minks from the blasting, he did not demand that the blasting stop. Foster, on the other hand, agreed to reduce the force of the blast.

(b) *Nature of Relationship:* The parties were neighbors and presumably intended to remain neighbors. Both businesses operated within a short distance from each other. The lumber company had been there for fifty years. The rancher operated an established business.

(c) *Nature of the Dispute:* This appears to be a short-term dispute. Blasting, the cause of the dispute, was done in order to build a road. Once it was built, the blasting would stop, but the acrimony attendant on a winner/loser resolution would perhaps poison the relationship forever.

(d) *Uncertainty of Legal Outcome:* Judicial decisions were divided as to whether the doctrine of absolute liability should apply where the damage from blasting was caused by concussion, vibration or jarring. The lack of decisive case law leaves both parties unsure of what might happen in court.

(e) *Desirability of a Private Settlement:* If this case arose today, Foster might be concerned with avoiding publicity and its possible attendant pressure from animal rights activist groups concerned with his treatment of the minks (i.e. keeping mink in steel cages in wood sheds). Foster could face boycotts and possibly demonstrations near his property which is located near a major highway. The company might also have an interest in a private settlement to avoid exposing its blasting operations.

B.   POSSIBLE MEDIATION APPROACHES

A.   By asking questions, the mediator could help the parties recognize the evidence which indicated that only during the whelping season is the mother mink disturbed by unaccustomed noises, and that regular and continuous noises such as the continuous noise from the highway do not disturb her. If the company were unwilling to put off the blasting for the six week whelping season, it might have agreed to blast more frequently using smaller shots of ammunition. Instead of twice a day using 50 pound charges, they could have blasted five times a day using 20 pound charges, or ten times using 10 pound charges. The noise would be continuous, but it would cause less vibration while the area would be cleared for road building. Both parties would be able to continue their business with minimal losses.

B. Another possible solution might have been for the parties to try to insulate the mother minks from the noise and the vibrations. Perhaps Foster could have traded some mink pelts in exchange for wood to reinforce and insulate the cages. This would certainly have minimized the vibrations.

C. It may also have been possible for Preston to warn Foster each time the blasting was to occur. According to the evidence, this was twice a day. In this way, the mothers could be isolated from the kittens during that time. Other solutions come to mind if the parties are aware of the potential problems before the whelping season begins, such as conditioning the minks, constructing special cages, etc.

MEDIATION BIBLIOGRAPHY

Binder, Bergman and Price, *Lawyers as Counselors: A Client–Centered Approach* (1991);

Binder and Price, *Legal Interviewing and Counseling: A Client–Centered Approach* (1977);

Burns, *The Enforceability of Mediated Agreements: An Essay on Legitimation and Process Integrity*, 2 Ohio St.J.Dis.Res. 93 (1986);

Bernstein, *The Desirability of a Statute for the Enforcement of Mediated Agreements,* 2 Ohio J. of Dispute Resolution 117 (1986);

Chaykin, *The Liabilities and Immunities of Mediators: A Hostile Environment for Model Legislation,* 2 Ohio St.J.Dis.Res. 47 (1986–87);

Folberg and Taylor, *Mediation A Comprehensive Guide to Resolving Conflicts Without Litigation* (1984);

Fuller, *Mediation—Its Forms and Functions,* 44 S.Cal.L.Rev. 305 (1971);

Mnookin & Kornhauser, *Bargaining in the Shadow of the Law: The Case of Divorce,* 88 Yale L.J. 950 (1979);

Moore, *The Mediation Process* (1986);

Murray, Rau and Sherman, Processes of Dispute Resolution: The Role of Lawyers, Chapter 3, Mediation, (1989);

Riskin, *Toward New Standards for the Neutral Lawyer in Mediation,* 26 Arizona L.Rev. 329 (1984);

Rogers and McEwen, *Mediation Law Policy Practice* (1989);

Rogers and Salem, *A Student's Guide to Mediation and the Law* (1987);

Simkin and Fidandis, *Mediation and the Dynamics of Collective Bargaining* 2nd edition (1986);

Stulberg, *Taking Charge/Managing Conflict* (1987).

CHAPTER 4
ARBITRATION
I. INTRODUCTION

Arbitration is the most formalized alternative to the court adjudication of disputes. In this process, disputing parties present their case to a neutral third party who is empowered to render a decision. Pragmatic and policy considerations have led courts and legislatures to endorse arbitration as the preferred process in resolving a wide range of disputes. As a result, arbitration has been transformed today into a flexible adjudicatory process, operating both in the mandatory, public context as well as in voluntary, private settings.

II. HISTORICAL PERSPECTIVE

There is nothing new about arbitration as a method of private adjudication in America. Commercial arbitration has flourished in this country since the 18th century even though the courts have not always looked kindly toward the arbitration process. No doubt the early American mistrust of arbitration was influenced by the English court's hostility as exemplified in Lord Coke's famous statement in *Vynior's Case* that arbitration agreements were against public policy because they "oust the jurisdiction" of the courts. The rationale for this judicial hostility is not entirely clear. Lord Campbell has suggested that it may have been based on economic interests since judges depended upon fees for their services. Or, it could simply be what the Second Circuit Court of Appeals has described as the "hypnotic power of the phrase, 'oust the jurisdiction.'" (*Kulukundis Shipping Co., S/A, v. Amtorg Trading Corporation* (1942)).

For a long period in American legal history the courts adopted the English courts' antagonism towards executory arbitration agreements and routinely refused to enforce contract clauses which required the arbitration of future disputes. If the parties did submit a dispute to the arbitration process, they were often permitted to withdraw before the arbitration decision was rendered.

Judicial attitudes toward arbitration began to change in the early twentieth century with the passage of state and federal statutes promoting arbitration. In 1920, New York became the first state to enact an arbitration statute giving parties the right to control future disputes as well as settle existing disputes through the arbitration process. The New York statute provided a model for the Uniform Arbitration Act of 1955 (UAA) (Appendix). Today, the majority of states have adopted arbitration statutes modeled on the UAA.

In 1925, Congress enacted the United States Arbitration Act, known today as the Federal Arbitration Act (FAA) (Appendix), 9 U.S.C.A. § 1 et seq., to place arbitration agreements on the same footing as other contracts and to encourage the use of commercial arbitration as an alternative to court. The FAA was intended to reverse centuries of judicial hostility towards the arbitration process. Section 2, the primary substantive provision of the Act, provides that a written agreement to arbitrate "in any maritime transaction or a contract evidencing a transaction involving commerce ... shall be valid, irrevocable, and enforceable, save upon such grounds as exist at law or in equity for the revocation of any contract." In effect, Section 2 created a body of federal substantive law of arbitrability, applicable to any arbitration agreement within the coverage of the Act.

The Act provides in Section 3 for a stay of proceedings in a case where a court is satisfied that the issue before it is arbitrable under the agreement. Section 4 of the Act directs a federal court to order parties to proceed to arbitration if there has been a "failure, neglect, or refusal of any party to honor an arbitration agreement."

Arbitration received increasing visibility after World War II with its expansion into the labor-management arena. In 1947, Congress passed the Labor–Management Relations Act (LMRA), popularly known as the Taft–Hartley Act, which established the National Labor Relations Board (NLRB) to arbitrate disputes regarding unfair labor practices. Four Supreme Court cases decided between

1957 and 1960 firmly established the favored position that arbitration would enjoy in effectuating national labor policy. Three out of the four cases arose under Section 301 of the Labor Management Relations Act.

In *Textile Workers Union v. Lincoln Mills* (1957), the Supreme Court held that an employer's promise to arbitrate grievances in a collective bargaining agreement was specifically enforceable under the federal common law of collective bargaining. The Court considered grievance arbitration provisions to be the *quid pro quo* for unions' non-strike agreements, and then connected labor arbitration to industrial harmony:

> Viewed in this light, the legislation does more than confer jurisdiction in the federal courts over labor organizations. It expresses a federal policy that federal courts should enforce these agreements on behalf of or against labor organizations and that industrial peace can be best obtained only in that way.

Three years later, in a series of cases, known as the "Steelworkers Trilogy," the Court gave more concrete shape to its policy of giving solemn deference to labor arbitration awards. The first Trilogy case, *United Steelworkers v. American Manufacturing Company* (1960) established the predominant role that arbitrators would play in the resolution of labor disputes:

> The function of the court is very limited when the parties have agreed to submit all questions of

contract interpretation to the arbitrator. It is confined to ascertaining whether the party seeking arbitration is making a claim which on its face is governed by the contract. Whether the moving party is right or wrong is a question of contract interpretation for the arbitrator.

In the second Trilogy case, *United Steelworkers v. Warrior & Gulf Navigation Co.* (1960) the Court continued to reflect a strong congressional policy favoring the resolution of labor disputes through the arbitration process. Consistent with this policy, the courts were to have a limited role interpreting the collective bargaining agreement:

... the judicial inquiry under Section 301 must be strictly confined to the question whether the reluctant party did agree to arbitrate .... An order to arbitrate the particular grievance should not be denied unless it may be said with positive assurance that the arbitration clause is not susceptible of an interpretation that covers the asserted dispute.

Finally, in *United Steelworkers v. Enterprise Wheel & Car Corp.* (1960) the Court again emphasized the preeminent role of arbitrators in interpreting the collective bargaining agreement. Courts would have no business second-guessing an arbitrator as long as the arbitration award "draws its essence from the collective bargaining agreement."

Until the early 1970's, arbitration jurisprudence developed chiefly from the use of arbitration in commercial transactions and labor agreements. Today, the subject matter of arbitration encompasses a much broader subject area to include: prisoners' rights, medical malpractice, consumer rights, intellectual property rights, and antitrust. The expansion of arbitration into these new contexts raises significant questions in civil justice reform and challenges policy-makers to effect these changes without diminishing the quality of justice.

III. THE TRADITIONAL MODEL OF ARBITRATION

The traditional model of arbitration contemplates a *voluntary* process where parties submit a dispute to a neutral person for a decision. It results from a contractual arrangement in which parties agree in advance of a dispute, or after a dispute has arisen, that arbitration will substitute for formal judicial proceedings.

In theory, traditional arbitration has numerous advantages over the litigation process, not necessarily because it is a superior form of justice, but simply because it uncomplicates the path to justice. Arbitration is generally considered a more efficient process than litigation because it is quicker and less expensive. Arbitration also offers greater flexibility of process and procedure than litigation. It is a private process which disputing parties have considerable latitude in shaping. The parties choose the arbitrators and exercise control over the relevant procedures. They decide the degree of formality which will govern and the extent to which the trappings of litigation, from pre-trial motions to discovery, are relevant.

Arbitrators typically have more expertise in the specific subject matter of the dispute than do judges. They also have greater flexibility in decision-making than judges since they are not bound by the principle of *stare decisis* in rendering a decision. In fact, arbitrators are not even required to give reasons to support their awards.

In practice, however, arbitration has been criticized on a number of grounds. First, efficiency may be lost when arbitration is conducted by a panel of arbitrators whose scheduling problems increase delay and costs. Second, some commentators argue that efficiency is achieved at the expense of the quality of justice and that the difficulty of appealing an arbitral award may give arbitrators a license to do injustice. Finally, in some areas, particularly labor relation cases, the increasing formality of arbitration hearings resembles aspects of the judicial system.

IV. COMPULSORY ARBITRATION

The growth of compulsory arbitration in the United States is not surprising given the current penchant for the arbitration process. The notion of *requiring* parties to arbitrate, however, is the antithesis of traditional arbitration with its emphasis on the voluntary agreement of the parties. Some of the most visible growth areas for mandatory arbitration are public sector employment disputes, court-annexed programs and medical malpractice disputes.

1. Public Sector Arbitration

Critical public sector employees such as the police, teachers and firefighters, are usually not permitted to participate in strikes as part of their labor negotiations. A majority of states, therefore, have enacted legislation requiring compulsory arbitration as the final step in negotiating the terms of a collective bargaining agreement between municipalities and their critical employees. These statutes typically provide for the arbitration of interest disputes by a tripartite panel of arbitrators who decide such issues as wages, hours and working conditions.

Judicial review of compulsory arbitration awards differs from review of traditional arbitration awards since there is usually a record of the arbitration hearing and a written decision from the arbitrator. Courts are therefore able to examine the awards to determine whether they are supported by substantial evidence in the record.

A major constitutional concern with compulsory arbitration statutes is that they delegate legislative power to independent arbitrators who are not accountable to the public for their decisions. This is a significant concern since many issues decided by these arbitrators ultimately involve political or legislative questions. While some state laws have been invalidated on the grounds of impermissible delegation of legislative power, the majority of courts have upheld the constitutionality of these statutes where there is reasonable criteria for the arbitration award.

2. Court–Annexed Arbitration

Several state and federal district courts have adopted court-annexed arbitration systems in an effort to reduce the delay and expense associated with the disposition of civil litigation. Court-annexed systems, also known as judicial arbitration, generally operate by diverting specific categories of civil cases to mandatory, arbitration. Some systems, however, are permissive and litigants are simply offered the option of arbitration. The arbitrations are usually conducted by attorneys or retired judges who have quasi-judicial powers.

The diversion of specified cases to arbitration is expected to result in expeditious settlements. In some cases, this may happen where the diversion acts as an incentive to a pre-hearing settlement. In other situations, the parties may accept the arbitrator's award or, the arbitrator's decision may act as a stimulus to negotiations between the parties. Attorneys are required to participate in good faith and risk sanctions for their failure to do so.

Court-annexed arbitration differs from the traditional arbitration model in a number of respects. It lacks the private and consensual attributes of traditional arbitration since it operates under the court's supervision. Litigants have the right to a trial *de novo* if they are not satisfied with the arbitrator's award. In some systems, however, litigants must pay court costs or arbitrators' fees if they do not better their position at trial. This of course is a disincentive to exercising a right to trial *de novo*.

Court-annexed programs have survived seventh amendment challenges as long as there are no substantial restrictions placed on the right to a jury trial. Courts typically find that the burden imposed on parties by compulsory arbitration is usually outweighed by the benefits of a speedy, less expensive and more efficient trial system. The leading case upholding the constitutionality of compulsory arbitration is *Application of Smith* (1955). A local court rule authorized compulsory arbitration in all cases involving claims less than $10,000.00. Responding to a challenge based on Pennsylvania's constitutional provisions for the right to a jury trial, the Pennsylvania Supreme Court held that:

> [t]he only purpose of the constitutional provision is to secure the right of trial by jury before rights of person or property are *finally* determined. All that is required is that the right of appeal for the purpose of presenting the issue to a jury must not be burdened by the imposition of onerous conditions, restrictions or regulations which would make the right practically unavailable.

A number of studies have been conducted on the effect of court-annexed arbitration on the quality of the justice system. While litigants generally perceive the system to be beneficial and fair, there is some dispute as to whether court-annexed arbitration significantly reduces judicial time and public costs. In fact, some commentators believe that the growing formality of these programs may actually increase costs and delays.

3. Medical Malpractice Arbitration

One response to the rising costs of medical malpractice lawsuits has been the diversion of these cases from tort litigation to compulsory arbitration. A great number of states have enacted statutes requiring the arbitration of medical malpractice disputes. Statutory approaches vary. Some states provide for mandatory non-binding arbitration as a pre-requisite for bringing a case to court. Often, as an adjunct to this process, parties are required to submit their cases to a screening panel, sometimes known as an arbitration board, whose function is to weed out frivolous lawsuits. Parties have the right to demand a trial *de novo* in state court if they find the arbitrator's award unacceptable.

Other states provide for voluntary but binding arbitration agreements which patients sign before receiving medical treatment. Since the arbitrator's award is final in these situations, it is important to show that the patient had knowledge that he or she was agreeing to arbitration. Otherwise, an arbitration agreement will be struck down as unconscionable.

V. ARBITRATION DEFINITIONS

1. Interest and Rights Arbitration

Arbitration in the labor-management area can be classified into two basic categories: "interests" arbitration and "rights" or grievance arbitration. "Interests" arbitration involves settling the terms of a contract between the parties. When impasse occurs, and parties are unable to agree on the terms of a contract, an arbitrator decides the terms. The use of "interests" arbitration is most common in public sector collective bargaining.

"Rights" arbitration, also known as grievance arbitration, concerns the violation or interpretation of an existing contract. The arbitrator issues a final decision regarding the meaning of the contract terms.

2. Final Offer Arbitration

There is a general assumption that arbitrators are susceptible of making compromise decisions in an effort to remain acceptable to both parties. Final offer arbitration militates against this tendency by requiring that parties submit their "final offer" to the arbitrator who may choose only one. This device gives each party an incentive to make a reasonable offer or risk that the arbitrator will accept the other party's offer. Final offer arbitration is used in baseball salary disputes and in public sector collective bargaining.

VI. LEGAL ISSUES

1. Arbitrability

The question of arbitrability focuses on whether a particular dispute is properly the subject of arbitration. There are two dimensions to this question: substantive and procedural. Substantive arbitrability is concerned with whether a particular subject matter was intended by the parties to be covered by their arbitration agreement. Since the traditional model of arbitration assumes a voluntary undertaking, a party cannot be required to submit a dispute to arbitration. Procedural arbitrability is concerned with whether the procedural requirements for arbitration, such as timeliness and specificity, have been satisfied.

(i) Substantive Arbitrability

The Court's language from the *Steelworkers Trilogy*, suggests a limited judicial role court in determining substantive arbitrability. In deciding whether to order or prevent an arbitration, the court's inquiry is limited "to ascertaining whether the party seeking arbitration is making a claim which on its face is governed by the contract." The court must order arbitration "unless it may be said with positive assurance that the arbitration clause is not susceptible of an interpretation that covers the dispute."

As the law of arbitration between private parties has developed, a difference in perspective has evolved between arbitration in commercial matters and arbitration in labor relations. Since the "Steelworkers Trilogy" in 1960, courts have recognized a presumption of arbitrability in labor disputes. In *AT & T Technologies, Inc. v. Communications Workers of America* (1986) the Court stated that this approach acknowledges the "greater institutional competence of arbitrators in interpreting collective bargaining agreements, [and] 'furthers the national labor policy of peaceful resolution of labor disputes and thus best accords with the parties' presumed objectives in pursuing collective bargaining.'"

On the other hand, the traditional rule with respect to commercial contracts does not recognize a presumption of arbitrability. Rather, the agreement to arbitrate must expressly and unequivocally encompass the subject matter of a particular dispute before a party can be forced to submit to arbitration. Some courts however, are beginning to apply a presumption of arbitrability in commercial contracts cases. In *Mitsubishi Motors Corporation v. Soler Chrysler–Plymouth* (1983) a commercial contract case, the court cited familiar language from the *Steelworkers Trilogy* favoring a presumption of arbitration: ". . . all doubts are resolved in favor of arbitration; arbitration will be ordered 'unless it may be said with positive assurance that the arbitration clause is not susceptible of an interpretation that covers the asserted dispute.' "

Labor management relations in the public sector raise somewhat different considerations on the question of arbitrability. Collective bargaining agreements between a public employer and employees are sufficiently different from private commercial and labor agreements that they cannot be categorized under either one of those headings. In the field of public employment, the public policy favoring arbitration does not yet carry the same historical or general acceptance as exists in the private sector. Parties to a collective bargaining agreement in the public sector may not wish to adopt a broad view of arbitrability. The New York Court of Appeals adopted a thoughtful approach in determining the question of arbitrability in this area, in a case arising under the Taylor Law which regulates labor management relations in New York's public sector. In this case, which involved a public school teacher's grievance, the court wrote:

"... [T]he threshold consideration by the courts as to whether there is a valid agreement to arbitrate must proceed in sequence on two levels. Initially it must be determined whether arbitration claims with respect to the particular subject matter are authorized by the terms of the Taylor Law. ... If it is concluded, however, that reference to arbitration is authorized under the Taylor Law, inquiry then turns at a second level to a determination of whether such authority was in fact exercised and whether the parties did agree by the terms of their particular arbitration clause to refer their differences in this specific area to arbitration. ...

Acting Superintendent of Schools of Liverpool Central School District v. United Liverpool Faculty Association (1977).

A subsequent amendment to New York's Education Law has eliminated arbitral review for teachers in cases arising out of adverse determinations by an Education Law hearing panel.

In recent years, substantive arbitrability has been a fertile source of litigation, particularly where statutory claims are involved. The Supreme Court has signalled strong support for the integrity of the arbitration process by upholding the enforceability of arbitration agreements arising under a wide range of federal statutes. The Court's rationale for endorsing arbitration is expressed in *Mitsubishi Motors Corp. v. Soler Chrysler–Plymouth, Inc.* (1985), a Sherman Act case in which the Court upheld the arbitrability of antitrust claims arising in an international commercial transaction:

By agreeing to arbitrate a statutory claim, a party does not forego the substantive rights afforded by the statute; it only submits to their resolution in an arbitral, rather than a judicial, forum. It trades the procedures and opportunity for review of the courtroom for the simplicity, informality, and expedition of arbitration.

In *Shearson/American Express v. McMahon* (1987) the Court upheld the arbitrability of claims

arising under the Securities Exchange Act of 1934
and the civil provisions of the Racketeer Influenced and Corrupt Organizations Act (RICO).
McMahon marked a significant departure from the
Court's anti-arbitration orientation exemplified in
Wilko v. Swan (1953). *Wilko,* one of the earliest
cases to address the arbitrability of statutory
claims and a frequently cited precedent for rejecting arbitrability, held that claims arising under
section 12(2) of the Securities Act of 1933 were not
subject to compulsory arbitration. The *Wilko*
court's mistrust of the arbitration process was
based on several considerations: arbitrators were
incapable of understanding the legal and factual
complexities of claims arising under the Securities
Act; arbitrators did not have to offer any reasons
for their awards; the power to vacate an award is
limited; and, an arbitrator's error in interpretation of law is not subject to judicial review.

The precedential value of *Wilko* was considerably weakened in *McMahon,* when the Court observed that the reasons for judicial hostility towards arbitration have subsequently been rejected
by the court as a basis for holding statutory claims
nonarbitrable. The *McMahon* Court established
the following framework for analysis in determining the enforceability of arbitration agreements
under the FAA. The FAA requires enforcement of
arbitration agreements. Congress can override
this mandate by precluding waiver of the judicial
forum for the exercise of the specific statutory
right at issue. But, the party opposing arbitration,
has the burden of demonstrating that Congress

intended to preclude waiver. Congressional intent may be found in the text or legislative history of the statute, or the "inherent conflict between arbitration and the statute's underlying purposes." The parties in *McMahon* failed to demonstrate that Congress intended to except from the FAA's coverage claims arising under RICO and the Exchange Act.

Wilko was finally overruled two years later, in *Rodriguez de Quijas v. Shearson/American Express, Inc.* (1989) when the Supreme Court upheld the enforceability of predispute agreements to arbitrate claims arising under the Securities Act of 1933. Writing for the majority, Justice Kennedy stated that "[I]t also would be undesirable for the decisions in *Wilko* and *McMahon* to continue to exist side by side."

The Supreme Court's enthusiastic endorsement of arbitration continued beyond the commercial context in *Gilmer v. Interstate/Johnson Lane Corp.* (1991), wherein the Court held that claims arising under the Age Discrimination in Employment Act (ADEA) can be subjected to compulsory arbitration pursuant to the FAA. Relying on the test enunciated in *McMahon,* the Court stated that a party would be held to his bargain to arbitrate unless he could show that Congress intended to preclude a waiver of a judicial forum for ADEA claims.

Robert Gilmer had been hired as a manager of financial services in 1981. In 1987, at the age of 62, his employment was terminated. As a condition of his employment, Gilmer had been required to sign an agreement to arbitrate any disputes between himself and his employer arising out of his employment or its termination.

Gilmer argued that compulsory arbitration of ADEA claims was inconsistent with the purposes of the ADEA. The Court, however, was not persuaded. In the Court's view, there is no inconsistency between the social policies furthered by the ADEA and enforcing agreements to arbitrate age discrimination claims. Just as arbitration focuses on specific disputes between the parties, so too does judicial dispute resolution. Both processes can further broader social purposes. The court noted that other laws such as the Sherman Act, the Securities Exchange Act of 1934, RICO and the Securities Act of 1933 are designed to further important public policies but claims under them are appropriate for arbitration.

Gilmer also argued that compulsory arbitration deprived claimants of the judicial forum provided for by the ADEA. The court rejected this argument noting that "Congress ... did not explicitly preclude arbitration or other non-judicial resolution of claims, even in its recent amendments to the ADEA." The Court likewise rejected Gilmer's challenge to the adequacy of arbitration procedures—the lack of written opinions, biased arbitration panels, limited discovery, noting that it had rejected most of these generalized attacks in its recent arbitration cases because they rested on an outmoded suspicion of the arbitral process.

Gilmer also argued that unequal bargaining power between employers and employees is sufficient reason not to enforce arbitration agreements related to ADEA claims. The Court responded, however, that "[M]ere inequality in bargaining power, ... is not a sufficient reason to hold that arbitration agreements are never enforceable in the employment context." In any event, the court found no indication of unfair bargaining power in this case and stated that such an argument was best left for resolution in specific cases.

Finally, Gilmer argued that three earlier employment decisions, *Alexander v. Gardner–Denver Co.* (1974) and its progeny, *Barrentine v. Arkansas–Best Freight System, Inc.* (1981) and *McDonald v. City of West Branch* (1984), (discussed in section VI *infra*) precluded arbitration of employment discrimination claims. The Court distinguished these cases on several grounds: they arose in the collective bargaining context; they involved contractual rights unlike this case which involved individual statutory rights; the issue in those cases related to the preclusive effects of an arbitration award and not the enforceability of an agreement to arbitrate statutory claims; and, finally, those cases were not decided under the FAA which has a liberal federal policy favoring arbitration.

If the latest round of Supreme Court arbitrability decisions is any indicator, an expansive, pro-arbitration view will probably continue to influence arbitration jurisprudence. Attorneys must therefore fully consider the implications of having their clients sign pre-dispute arbitration agreements.

(ii) Procedural Arbitrability

Questions related to procedural arbitrability are reserved to arbitrators. Generally, these questions are closely connected to the substantive merits of the dispute and it makes little sense to have them decided in different forums. Thus, arbitrators' decisions on procedural questions will receive the same judicial deference as their decisions on the merits of the dispute.

The Supreme Court specifically addressed the question of procedural arbitrability in *John Wiley & Sons, Inc. v. Livingston* (1964), and acknowledged the specialized competence of arbitrators to resolve procedural issues. *Wiley* involved an action under Section 301 of the Labor Management Relations Act, to compel arbitration under a collective bargaining agreement. The specific question before the Court was whether the court or an arbitrator should decide if arbitration provisions in a collective-bargaining contract survived a corporate merger so as to bind the surviving corporation. The Court had "no doubt" that this question should be decided by the courts but held that once the court makes a determination that the parties are obligated to submit a dispute to arbitration, then "procedural" questions arising out of the dispute should be left to the arbitrator.

2. Separability

The issue of separability arises when there is a challenge to the validity of an arbitration clause because the overall contract is invalid. The claim may be that the entire contract is void because of such defects as fraud in the inducement, lack of a meeting of the minds, or lack of mutuality of consideration. The crucial question raised by such claims is whether the court or the arbitrator should resolve them?

The federal rule of separability enunciated by the Supreme Court in *Prima Paint Corp. v. Flood & Conklin Mfg. Co.* (1967), allows arbitrators to resolve such claims unless they are related to the arbitration clause itself. *Prima Paint* involved a claim of fraud in the inducement of a contract governed by the FAA. Flood & Conklin (F & C) agreed both to perform consulting services for and not compete with Prima Paint. The contract contained a broad arbitration clause which provided that " '[a]ny controversy or claim arising out of or relating to this Agreement ... shall be settled by arbitration in the City of New York, ..." F & C sent Prima Paint a notice requesting arbitration on the grounds that Prima had failed to make a payment under the contract. Prima brought an action in federal court to rescind the entire agreement on the grounds of fraud. The alleged fraud consisted of F & C's misrepresentation at the time the contract was made, that it was solvent, when in fact, it was insolvent. F & C moved to stay Prima's lawsuit pending arbitration of the fraud issue. The lower courts held that the action should be stayed to permit arbitration of the issue. The Second Circuit Court of Appeals held that a claim of fraud in the inducement is not for the court, but for the arbitrator to decide and called this a rule of "national substantive law." The Supreme Court adopted a broad view of severability:

> [A]rbitration clauses as a matter of federal law are 'separable' from the contracts in which they are embedded, and ... where no claim is made that fraud was directed to the arbitration clause itself, a broad arbitration clause will be held to encompass arbitration of the claim that the contract itself was induced by fraud.

While the Court's holding in *Prima* extended only to the specific issue of fraud in the inducement, federal courts and a majority of state courts have expanded its principle to include other defects, consistent with a liberal regard for the federal policy favoring arbitration.

3. Federalism Issues

The FAA was enacted during the era of *Swift v. Tyson* when federal courts were free to fashion general federal common law for questions not governed by state statutes. After the Supreme

Court's decision in *Erie Railroad Co. v. Tompkins* in 1938, a number of questions arose regarding the application of the *Erie* doctrine to the FAA. Many of these questions related to whether the FAA should be treated as substantive law under *Erie*. The following section identifies the leading Supreme Court cases in this area. A number of them show strong support for a federal policy of upholding arbitration agreements despite state substantive or procedural policies which may conflict.

(a) *Bernhardt v. Polygraphic Co.* (1956), a diversity case, involved an application for a stay of litigation pending arbitration. The Supreme Court made it clear that enforcement of arbitration clauses under Section 2 of the FAA was substantive for purposes of the *Erie* doctrine. *Bernhardt* was an action for damages resulting from discharge under an employment contract made in New York between a New York corporation and a New York resident. The petitioner later became a resident of Vermont where he was to perform his duties.

The contract provided that in case of any dispute the parties would submit the matter to arbitration under New York law. The district court ruled that under *Erie*, the arbitration provision of the contract was governed by Vermont law which held that arbitration contracts were revocable at any time prior to the issuance of an arbitral award. The Supreme Court ruled that the arbitration contract at issue fell outside the provisions of section 2 of the FAA because the contract was neither a maritime transaction nor a transaction in commerce.

(b) *Prima Paint Corp. v. Flood & Conklin Mfg. Co.* (1967). The facts of this case are discussed in the previous section on separability. With respect to federalism issues, one of the arguments which had been raised in *Prima Paint* was that under the *Erie* doctrine, federal courts were bound to follow state law which called for a different result on the disputed issue in that case. The Supreme Court responded as follows:

> The question in this case, however, is not whether Congress may fashion federal substantive rules to govern questions arising in simple diversity cases ... Rather, the question is whether Congress may prescribe how federal courts are to conduct themselves with respect to the subject matter over which Congress plainly has power to legislate. The answer to that can only be in the affirmative.

(c) *Moses H. Cone Memorial Hospital v. Mercury Construction Corp.* (1983). The Court stated in *Moses H. Cone,* that the substantive law created by the FAA was applicable in state and federal courts. The factual background of this case involved a contract dispute between a hospital and a building contractor. Their agreement provided that disputes could be submitted by either party to binding arbitration. After a dispute arose, the hospital filed an action in state court seeking a declaratory judgment that the contractor had no right to arbitration. In response, the contractor filed a diversity suit in federal district court seeking an order compelling arbitration under Section 4 of the FAA. The district court stayed the action out of deference to the parallel state court litigation. The Fourth Circuit reversed and remanded the case with instructions to order arbitration.

The Supreme Court considered the propriety of the district court's decision to stay the federal suit and found no showing of "exceptional circumstances" to justify the stay. The Court concluded, therefore, that the stay frustrated the FAA's policy of "rapid and unobstructed enforcement of arbitration agreements." The language of *Moses H. Cone* clearly expresses what had simply been implied in *Prima Paint* that:

Section 2 is a congressional declaration of a liberal federal policy favoring arbitration agreements, notwithstanding any state substantive or procedural policies to the contrary. The effect of the section is to create a body of federal substantive law of arbitrability, applicable to any arbitration agreement within the coverage of the Act.

(d) In *Southland Corp. v. Keating* (1984) the Court invalidated a state law which undercut the enforceability of arbitration agreements. The facts in *Southland Corp.* involved the constitutionality of a section of the California Franchise Investment Law which invalidated certain arbitration agreements covered by the FAA. Southland Corp., the owner and franchisor of 7–eleven convenience stores and several 7–eleven franchisees had an agreement with a clause requiring arbitration of any controversy or claim arising out of or relating to the franchise agreement. Several of the franchisees filed actions against Southland in the California Superior Court, alleging fraud, misrepresentation, breach of contract, breach of fiduciary duty, and violation of the disclosure requirements of the California Franchise Investment Law. These actions were consolidated into a class action and Southland moved to compel arbitration in accordance with the contract. The California Superior Court ordered arbitration of all claims except those based upon the Franchise Investment Law. The appeals court reversed and the California Supreme Court upheld the decision.

Relying on its earlier pronouncements in *Prima Paint,* and *Moses H. Cone,* that the FAA created a body of federal substantive law that is applicable in both state and federal courts, the Court held that the California law violated the Supremacy clause and was therefore, invalid.

(e) In *Dean Witter Reynolds, Inc. v. Byrd* (1984) the Supreme Court held that the FAA requires federal courts to enforce agreements to arbitrate, even if this results in "piecemeal litigation." The facts of this case involved an investor who signed a Customer's Agreement with Dean Witter Reynolds which provided that any controversy would be settled by arbitration. After the value of his account declined substantially, the investor filed a complaint against Dean Witter in federal court alleging various violations of the Securities Exchange Act of 1934 and of various state law provisions. Dean Witter filed a motion for an order severing the pendent state-law claims, compelling their arbitration, and staying arbitration of those claims pending resolution of the federal-court action. The district court denied the motion to sever and the appeals court affirmed.

The Court's opinion in *Byrd* makes it clear that the FAA is not simply a quick fix dispute resolution vehicle but rather a mechanism for the enforcement of private arbitration agreements:

> The preeminent concern of Congress in passing the Act was to enforce private agreements into which parties had entered, and that concern requires that we rigorously enforce agreements to arbitrate, even if the result is "piecemeal" litigation, at least absent a countervailing policy manifested in another federal statute .... By compelling arbitration of state-law claims, a district court successfully protects the contractual rights of the parties and their rights under the Arbitration Act.

(f) *Volt Information Sciences, Inc. v. Board of Trustees of Leland Stanford Junior University* (1989). *Volt* marks a detour in the expansive judicial interpretation of the FAA with the Court's refusal to extend that federal law where the parties had agreed to be governed by state arbitration rules. The case arose out of a construction contract between a university and a contractor. One of the contract provisions called for arbitration of all disputes between the parties "arising out of or relating to this contract or the breach thereof." The contract also had a choice-of-law clause providing that "the Contract shall be governed by the law of the place where the Project is located." A dispute over compensation arose and the contractor made a formal demand for arbitration. The university responded by filing an action against the contractor in California Supreme Court alleging fraud and breach of contract and seeking indemnification from two other companies involved in the project, with whom it did not have arbitration agreements. The contractor moved to compel arbitration and the university moved to stay the arbitration pursuant to a California rule which permits a court to stay arbitration pending resolution of related litigation between a party to the arbitration agreement and third parties not bound by it.

The Supreme Court acknowledged its prior holdings on the preemptive effect of the FAA, but held that in this case the FAA did not preempt California law since the parties had agreed to abide by state rules on arbitration. California law, which the parties had agreed would govern, permits a court to stay arbitration pending resolution of related litigation involving third parties not bound by the arbitration agreement.

4. Adhesion Contracts

The issue of adhesion typically arises when a standardized contract, prepared by a party with superior bargaining strength, is given to another party on a "take it or leave it" basis. The weaker party usually has very little choice regarding its terms.

Adhesion may arise in a variety of contexts in arbitration: pre-dispute arbitration agreements, clauses requiring arbitration before biased panels, contract provisions mandating arbitration of certain medical malpractice claims. Adhesion clauses lack true voluntariness and thus offend the traditional model of arbitration which requires that parties voluntarily assume a contractual undertaking to arbitrate their disputes.

Arbitration agreements with adhesive characteristics will be set aside unless they satisfy what one court has labeled "minimum levels of integrity." For example, in *Graham v. Scissor–Tail, Inc.* (1981), the Supreme Court of California invalidated a standardized contract between a music promoter and musical group where one of the contract provisions required arbitration of disputes before the musician's union. The court considered the union to be presumptively biased in favor of one party and held the contract unconscionable and unenforceable.

It should be noted, however, that litigants may have difficulty avoiding predispute arbitration agreements solely on the grounds of unequal bargaining power. In *Gilmer v. Interstate/Johnson Lane Corp.* a case arising under the Age Discrimination in Employment Act, the Supreme Court stated that "[M]ere inequality of bargaining power is not a sufficient reason to hold that arbitration agreements are never enforceable in the employment context." The Court cited its earlier holdings in *Rodriguez de Quijas* and *McMahon* which upheld the arbitrability of agreements between securities dealers and investors even though the relationship between those parties "... may involve unequal bargaining power." Relying on *Mitsubishi*, the Court indicated that in order for arbitration agreements to be set aside, litigants would have to establish "... well-supported claims that the agreement to arbitrate resulted from the sort of fraud or overwhelming economic power that would provide grounds 'for the revocation of any contract.'"

VII. THE ARBITRATION PROCEEDING

1. Provisional Relief

Provisional relief is a short-term remedy ordered by a court before a case is finally adjudicated on the merits. It is not uncommon for parties to a commercial arbitration agreement to seek such remedies as an injunction or attachment in order to maintain the status quo pending arbitration. The value of provisional relief in disputes was recognized by the Supreme Court in *Boys Markets, Inc. v. Retail Clerk's Union, Local 770* (1970), a case arising under Section 301 of the Labor Management Relations Act (LMRA):

> [t]he injunction ... is so important a remedial device, particularly in the arbitration context, that its availability or nonavailability in various courts will not only produce rampant forum shopping and maneuvering from one court to another but will also greatly frustrate any relative uniformity in the enforcement of arbitration agreements.

It should be noted that in Section 4 of the Norris–LaGuardia Act, 29 U.S.C.A. § 104, there is an explicit ban against preliminary injunctions pending arbitration of labor disputes. The Supreme Court's decision in *Boys Market* recognized that Section 301 of the LMRA contains a narrow exception to Section 4 of the Norris–LaGuardia Act.

The FAA gives little guidance on the availability of provisional remedies. Section 8 of the Federal Arbitration Act permits admiralty arbitration to begin by libel and seizure of the ship or other property of the opposing party. Otherwise, however, the FAA is silent regarding the ancillary power of a federal court to act, once it determines that a dispute is arbitrable. The Uniform Arbitration Act upon which many state arbitration statutes is based, omits any reference to allowing courts to order prejudgment relief.

Despite the statutory silence, most courts permit provisional relief to maintain the status quo pending arbitration. Courts have adopted a variety of approaches when determining whether to grant injunctions pending arbitration. Some courts apply traditional equitable analysis, examining the four factors which are used for all other preliminary injunctions. The plaintiff must demonstrate: (a) irreparable harm if injunctive relief is not granted; (b) likelihood of success on the merits; (c) that the potential harm to the plaintiff outweighs the harm suffered by the defendant; and (d) that the public interest will not be harmed if the court grants the injunction. e.g., *Teradyne, Inc. v. Mostek Corporation* (1986).

Other courts analyze the language of the contract containing the arbitration clause and grant a preliminary injunction only if the language requires the parties to maintain the status quo pending the resolution of any disputes. e.g., *RGI, Inc. v. Tucker & Associates, Inc.* (1988). Still, other courts grant a preliminary injunction if arbitration would not be able to compensate the parties for any injury incurred before the arbitrator rendered his decision. e.g., *Merrill Lynch, Pierce, Fenner & Smith, Inc. v. Bradley* (1985).

2. Initiating Arbitration

Arbitration may be initiated pursuant to a contractual provision or as a result of an ad hoc agreement to arbitrate. The agreement may be quite specific and provide for such concerns as the selection of the arbitrator, administration of the hearing, procedural rules and substantive law. If these details are not covered in the agreement or there is an ad hoc agreement to arbitrate, the parties may turn to specific agencies which administer arbitration.

Generally, a party would notify another party of her intent to arbitrate by sending a written demand for arbitration. (Appendix) The demand would identify the parties, describe the dispute and the type of relief which is claimed. While the demand need not comply with the formalities of a complaint in a civil action, it must be sufficiently clear to inform the opposing party of the specific issues to be arbitrated. A form for a demand in a commercial arbitration case is included in the appendix. The opposing party would usually respond in writing, indicating whether it believed the dispute was arbitrable.

3. Selection of Arbitrators

Assuming that the disputing parties agree that their dispute is arbitrable, they will begin the arbitrator selection process. Generally, arbitrations are conducted by one arbitrator. It is not uncommon however, to have a panel of three arbitrators, two of whom would be chosen by the parties and a third who would be appointed by a joint decision of the party-selected arbitrators. Other methods for selecting arbitrators are included in the Uniform Arbitration Act, the FAA and various state arbitration statutes and agency rules. In the labor field, parties to a collective bargaining agreement might designate a permanent arbitrator in their original contract.

(i) Qualifications of the Arbitrator

The personal qualifications of arbitrators include: honesty, integrity, impartiality and general competence in the subject matter of the dispute. Beyond these general requirements, arbitration practice is generally an open field. Some systems however, such as court-annexed arbitration, require that attorneys serve as arbitrators.

Since arbitrators act in a quasi-judicial capacity, they are held to the same high standards of impartiality by which judges are bound. In general, this means that arbitrators must avoid both the appearance and reality of conflict of interest and should uphold the integrity and fairness of the arbitration process. They should conform their conduct to the relevant code of ethics such as the Code of Professional Responsibility for Arbitrators of Labor–Management Disputes or the Code of Ethics for Arbitrators in Commercial Disputes (Appendix).

(ii) Arbitral Immunity

Both state and federal courts recognize that arbitrators enjoy quasi-judicial immunity from legal liability for actions taken in their arbitral capacity. This principle has also been observed in the international commercial setting. Arbitral immunity is justified with the same policy justifications that apply to judicial immunity namely, that arbitrators perform an important societal function and therefore need to be protected from reprisals that could have a negative impact on their adjudicatory powers. The rationale for this principle, expressed long ago by the Massachusetts Supreme Judicial Court in *Hoosac Tunnel Dock & Elevator Co. v. O'Brien* (1884), continues to influence the courts today:

> An arbitrator is a quasi judicial officer, under our laws, exercising judicial functions. There is as much reason in his case for protecting and insuring his impartiality, independence, and freedom from undue influences, as in the case of a judge or juror. The same considerations of public policy apply, and we are of opinion that the same immunity extends to him.

(iii) Testimonial Immunity

As a general rule, an arbitrator enjoys testimonial immunity and may not be required to testify regarding the merits of an award. There are, however, exceptions to this rule. For example, an arbitrator's testimony is permitted to show the fact that particular issues were submitted to arbitration for a decision. An arbitrator may also testify as to wrongful acts by one of the parties to the arbitration or even by other arbitrators on the panel.

4. The Arbitration Hearing

The requirements for the arbitration hearing vary from state to state but generally the hearing is similar in many respects to a trial. Both parties make opening statements and present their case to a neutral third party. Case presentations may include witnesses, documentation, and site inspections. The parties make closing arguments and may be required to submit briefs and memoranda in support of their position before the neutral renders a decision. The form of the hearings is essentially decided by the parties who often times will agree to abide by the rules of the agency which is administering the arbitration.

The arbitration process is different from the formality of litigation and trial in a number of respects. Arbitral factfinding is generally not equivalent to judicial factfinding. The record of the arbitration proceedings is not as complete. Written transcripts are usually unnecessary unless the parties decide to order them. The usual evidentiary rules are not applicable as the arbitrator has considerable discretion in the admission of evidence. Finally, rights such as discovery, compulsory process, cross-examination, and testimony under oath, are often limited.

5. Law Applied by the Arbitrator

The extent to which arbitrators should follow and apply substantive law remains unclear. The

Uniform Arbitration Act, Federal Arbitration Act and state statutes are silent on the application of law by the arbitrator. This is not surprising for, as the Supreme Court has observed, the majority of arbitrators are not lawyers and the specialized competence of arbitrators relates to "the law of the shop not the law of the land."

Certainly, the parties are free to specify in the arbitration clause, what rules of law will be applicable and the arbitrator is bound to honor their request. Without such direction however, the arbitrators are not bound by any uniform approach but only by their sense of justice. A study of commercial arbitration conducted several years ago by Professor Soia Mentschikoff attests to this approach. In her study, arbitrators were asked about their use of substantive rules of law in deciding cases. Eighty per cent of the arbitrators responded that they thought they should exercise decision-making power within the context of the principles of substantive law. At the same time, however, more than ninety per cent of these same arbitrators, thought that they could ignore substantive law if the interests of justice required it.

VIII. THE ARBITRATION AWARD

1. Judicial Review of the Arbitration Award

The courts take a narrow view of their role in reviewing arbitration awards. Significantly, errors of fact or law are not reviewable. The FAA lists four grounds on which an award may be vacated.

(a) Where the award was procured by corruption, fraud, or undue means.

(b) Where there was evident partiality or corruption in the arbitrators, or either of them.

(c) Where the arbitrators were guilty of misconduct in refusing to postpone the hearing, upon sufficient cause shown, or in refusing to hear evidence pertinent and material to the controversy; or of any other misbehavior by which the rights of any party have been prejudiced.

(d) Where the arbitrators exceeded their powers, or so imperfectly executed them that a mutual, final, and definite award upon the subject matter submitted was not made.

Case law has offered additional limited grounds for vacating an arbitrators award. Dictum from the now overruled Supreme Court decision, *Wilko v. Swan* (1953) suggests that an award may be set aside if it is in "manifest disregard of the law." This term was never defined by the Supreme Court but a useful definition appears in *Merrill Lynch, Pierce, Fenner & Smith, Inc. v. Bobker* (1986).

The [arbitrator's] error must have been obvious and capable of being readily and instantly perceived by the average person qualified to serve as an arbitrator. Moreover, the term 'disregard' implies that the arbitrator appreciates the existence of a clearly governing legal principle but decides to ignore or pay no attention to it.

Arbitration awards may also be vacated on public policy grounds but the scope of review in such cases is limited to well defined policy based on legal precedent and is not simply based on speculative interests. The Supreme Court emphasized its commitment to this rule in *United Paperworkers International Union v. Misco, Inc.* (1987) when it reversed a federal court decision which set aside an arbitrator's award on public policy grounds.

> ... a court's refusal to enforce an arbitrator's interpretation of such contracts is limited to situations where the contract as interpreted would violate "some explicit public policy" that is "well defined and dominant, and is to be ascertained 'by reference to the laws and legal precedents and not from general considerations of supposed public interests.' " ... [authorities omitted.]

Knowledge of the factual background in *Misco* is useful in understanding the depth of the Court's ruling. A Misco employee, Isiah Cooper, was discharged for allegedly violating his employer's drug rules. The employee had been found in the back seat of an automobile belonging to another person with a lighted marijuana cigarette in the front seat ashtray. The employee was then fired for violating the company rule against marijuana use on plant premise and he filed a grievance. Shortly before the arbitration hearing, the employer learned that the police searched the employees car on the same day he had been found in the car with the marijuana cigarette and found gleanings of marijuana.

After a hearing the arbitrator upheld the grievance and directed the employer to reinstate the employee with backpay and full seniority. The arbitrator refused to accept into evidence the fact that marijuana had been found in the employee's car on company property because the employer did not know of this fact when the employee was discharged and thus did not rely on it as a basis for the discharge.

The Company filed an action in district court seeking to vacate the arbitration award on several grounds, one of which was that ordering reinstatement of Cooper was contrary to public policy. The district court vacated the arbitration award and the Court of Appeals affirmed.

The Supreme Court reversed, holding that the Court of Appeals' public policy formulation was inadequate. Even if it were acceptable however, the Court concluded that no violation of that policy was demonstrated in this case.

2. Punitive Damages

Punitive or exemplary damages may be defined as those which exceed compensatory damages and which are awarded to punish a person for outrageous conduct. Public policy disfavors granting punitive awards which in most states requires a finding of some type of moral culpability.

Courts are divided on whether arbitrators should be allowed to award punitive sanctions. Generally, punitive damages are disfavored in labor arbitration unless the collective bargaining agreement specifically provides for them. Labor arbitration usually involves parties who have an on-going relationship, and it is thought that awarding punitive damages in this context could undercut the parties confidence in the arbitration process.

Less consensus exists, however, with respect to commercial arbitration. In contrast to labor arbitration, it is normally a short-term endeavor where the parties have chosen arbitration, not as a means of ongoing dispute resolution, but simply as an efficient means of resolving disputes. There are basically three views on awarding punitive damages in commercial arbitration cases. The first approach rejecting punitive damages awards is exemplified in *Garrity v. Lyle Stuart, Inc.* (1976) wherein the New York Court of Appeals held that permitting arbitrators to have this power violates public policy by displacing the court and jury as controllers of social sanctions.

A second approach holds that punitive damages can be awarded in commercial cases only if the parties' agreement specifically provides for that possibility. Finally, a growing minority of courts holds that broad arbitration clauses give arbitrators the power to award punitive damages, consistent with the strong federal policy in favor of upholding an arbitrator's ability to fashion appropriate remedies.

This issue may finally be resolved one day by the Supreme Court. Some authorities believe that the Court already hinted its approval of allowing punitive damages in securities arbitration cases when in *Shearson/American Express, Inc. v. McMahon* (1987), it held that RICO claims were arbitrable despite statutory treble damages.

3. Res Judicata, Collateral Estoppel and Arbitration

Arbitration's significant expansion raises critical questions concerning the preclusive effects of an arbitrator's decision in litigation arising from disputes that have been resolved in a prior arbitration. Under the doctrine of res judicata, also known as claim preclusion, a final judgment on the merits of an action precludes the parties or their privies from relitigating issues that were or could have been raised in that action. Collateral estoppel, also known as issue preclusion, applies to a subsequent suit between the parties on a different cause of action. Once a court has decided an issue of fact or law necessary to its judgment, that decision may preclude relitigation of the issue in a suit on a different cause of action involving a party to the first case. These doctrines developed at common law to relieve parties of the transaction costs associated with multiple lawsuits, and to promote finality and judicial economy by bringing an end to litigation.

It is well-settled that the doctrines of res judicata and collateral estoppel apply to arbitration awards. Section 84 of the *Restatement (Second) of Judgments* provides:

(1) . . . a valid and final award by arbitration has the same effects under the rules of res judicata, subject to the same exceptions and qualifications, as a judgment of a court.

(2) An award by arbitration with respect to a claim does not preclude relitigation of the same or a related claim based on the same transaction if a scheme of remedies permits assertion of the second claim notwithstanding the award regarding the first claim.

(3) A determination of an issue in arbitration does not preclude relitigation of that issue if:

(a) According preclusive effect to determination of the issue would be incompatible with a legal policy or contractual provision that the tribunal in which the issue subsequently arises be free to make an independent determination of the issue in question, or with a purpose of the arbitration agreement that the arbitration be specially expeditious; or

(b) The procedure leading to the award lacked the elements of adjudicatory procedure prescribed in § 83(2).

(4) If the terms of an agreement to arbitrate limit the binding effect of the award in another adjudication or arbitration proceeding, the extent to which the award has conclusive effect is determined in accordance with that limitation.

In recent years the Supreme Court has limited the claim and issue preclusion effects of arbitral awards where employees' federal statutory rights have been implicated under Title VII of the 1964 Civil Rights Act, the Fair Labor Standards Act and 42 U.S.C. section 1983. The three major cases in this area are discussed below:

(a) In *Alexander v. Gardner–Denver Co.* (1974) the Court considered the preclusive effect of an arbitral award in connection with an employee's statutory right to a trial de novo under Title VII. The factual background involved a discharged employee who filed a grievance under a collective-bargaining agreement which contained a broad arbitration clause. The employee also claimed that his discharge resulted from racial discrimination and he filed a racial discrimination complaint with the Colorado Civil Rights Commission. This was referred to the Equal Employment Opportunity Commission. Following an arbitration hearing at which the arbitrator held that his discharge was for cause and an EEOC determination that there was no reasonable ground to believe that a Title VII violation had occurred, the employee brought an action in district court alleging that his discharge resulted from racial discrimination. The district court granted Gardner–Denver's motion for summary judgment holding that the employee was bound by the prior arbitral decision and had no right to sue under Title VIII. The Court of Appeals affirmed. The Supreme Court reversed and declined to adopt a preclusion rule on the theory that the employee was asserting a statutory right "independent" of the arbitration process and was not seeking review of the arbitrator's decision.

Writing for the majority, Justice Powell opined that while the informality of arbitration procedures are well-suited to resolve contractual disputes, they are "inappropriate" to resolve Title VII rights. Arbitration was considered by the Court to be inferior to the judicial process in resolving Title VII claims because of the familiar laundry list of arbitration deficiencies:

> . . . the specialized competence of arbitrators pertains primarily to the law of the shop, not the law of the land . . . authorities omitted . . . the factfinding process in arbitration usually is not equivalent to judicial factfinding. The record of the arbitration proceedings is not as complete; the usual rules of evidence do not apply; and rights and procedures common to civil trials, such as discovery, compulsory process, cross-examination, and testimony under oath, are often severely limited or unavailable.

(b) In *Barrentine v. Arkansas–Best Freight System, Inc.* (1981) the Supreme Court again declined to defer to an arbitral decision where an employee's claim was based on rights arising out of the Fair Labor Standards Act [FLSA], a statute which was designed to provide minimum substantive protections to individual workers. The Court offered two rationales to support its denial of preclusion in this case. First, even if the employee had a meritorious claim, his union might decide for good reason not to support the claim strongly in arbitration. Second, even assuming that the union fairly presents the employee's wage claims, statutory rights might still not be adequately protected. Since arbitrators must follow the intent of the parties, rather than enforce the statute, they could issue rulings that were against the public policy underlying the FLSA.

(c) In *McDonald v. City of West Branch* (1984) the Supreme Court relied on its earlier holdings in *Alexander v. Gardner–Denver Co.* and *Barrentine v. Arkansas–Best Freight System, Inc.* and denied preclusive effect to an unappealed arbitration award in an action arising under 42 U.S.C.A. § 1983. Gary McDonald was discharged from the police force and filed a grievance pursuant to the collective bargaining agreement between the City of West Branch and the union, contending that there was "no proper cause" for his discharge. The grievance was taken to arbitration and the arbitrator ruled against McDonald. Subsequently, McDonald filed an action under 42 U.S.C.A. § 1983 against the city and certain officials including the Chief of Police, alleging that he was discharged for exercising his First Amendment rights. A jury returned a verdict against the Chief of Police which was reversed by the Court of Appeals. The Court of Appeals found that the arbitration process had not been abused and that McDonald's First Amendment claims were barred by res judicata and collateral estoppel.

The Supreme Court reversed the Court of Appeals and offered four reasons why judicial dispute resolution was preferable to arbitration in section 1983 cases. First, an arbitrator may not have the expertise to resolve the complex legal questions that arise in these cases. Second, an arbitrator may not have the authority to enforce section 1983 because his authority is derived solely from the contract. Third, the union may not make a vigorous presentation of the employee's case in arbitration. Finally, arbitral factfinding is less comprehensive than judicial factfinding.

IX. INTERNATIONAL ARBITRATION AGREEMENTS

Arbitration is a favored method of resolving international commercial disputes for the same reason that it is appealing on the domestic front: speed, low cost, privacy, expertise of the decisionmaker and procedural flexibility. At the international level, arbitration has additional advantages which include avoiding the unknown in a foreign courtroom and obtaining jurisdiction over foreign parties. The United Nations Committee on International Trade Law (UNCITRAL) and the International Chamber of Commerce have both established arbitration rules which enjoy widespread international acceptance.

International arbitration law in the United States is governed by both state and federal statutes. At the federal level, the FAA applies to contracts involving interstate and foreign commerce, as well as maritime transactions. Chapter 2 of the FAA has provisions which implement the United Nations Convention on the Recognition and Enforcement of Foreign Arbitral Awards, also known as the "New York Convention." This significant international agreement to which the United States is a party, provides for the recognition of arbitration agreements and for the enforcement of foreign arbitral awards. Article III provides:

> [e]ach Contracting State shall recognize arbitral awards as binding and enforce them in accordance with the rules of procedure of the territory where the award is relied upon, under the conditions laid down in the following articles. There shall not be imposed substantially more onerous conditions or higher fees or charges on the recognition or enforcement of arbitral awards to which this Convention applies than are imposed on the recognition or enforcement of domestic arbitral awards.

At the state level, every state has enacted its own arbitration statute which applies to intrastate arbitrations. In recent years, a number of states have enacted laws specifically governing international arbitration in an effort to create a hospitable climate for international commerce and trade. Many of these statutes are much more detailed than the FAA and include provisions for such items as jurisdiction, choice of law, grounds for challenging the arbitrators, and arbitrator appointment procedure. Some states have drafted their statutes in accordance with the Model Law on International Commercial Arbitration drafted by UNCITRAL.

Arbitration Bibliography

F. Elkouri & E. Elkouri, *How Arbitration Works,* (4th ed. 1985);

Hirshman, *"The Second Arbitration Trilogy: The Federalization of Arbitration Law,"* 71 Va.L.Rev. 1305 (1985);

Kanowitz, *"Alternative Dispute Resolution and the Public Interest: The Arbitration Experience,"* 38 Hastings Law J. 239 (1987);

G. Katsoris, *"Punitive Damages in Securities Arbitration: The Tower of Babel Revisited,"* 18 Ford. Urb.L.J. 573 (1991);

S. Mentschikoff, *Commercial Arbitration,* 61 Col. L.Rev. 846 (1961);

D. Nolan, *Labor Arbitration Law and Practice in a Nutshell* (1979);

G. Wilner, *Domke on Commercial Arbitration*
(1984).

CHAPTER 5

DISPUTE RESOLUTION IN THE COURT SYSTEM

The on-going institutionalization of ADR within the justice system offers litigants the opportunity to resolve disputes in a broader systems framework than the litigation process. Courts today are making greater use of the negotiation, mediation and arbitration processes through judicial settlement conferences (Chapter 2 Negotiation), court-annexed mediation (Chapter 3 Mediation) and arbitration (Chapter 4 Arbitration) programs. Newer mechanisms such as the summary jury trial and early neutral evaluation programs, as well as more innovative uses of magistrates, special masters and neutral experts use third parties to facilitate negotiation and help manage cases in an efficient and responsive manner. In short, the full panoply of judicial ADR developments shows federal and state court systems struggling to meet the demands for qualitative and quantitative justice.

I. THE SUMMARY JURY TRIAL

1. Overview

The summary jury trial (SJT) facilitates settlement by giving lawyers and their clients an advance assessment of what a jury might do in a given case. It is a nonbinding process in which lawyers present a brief synopsis of their case to a jury which then renders a non-binding, advisory decision. After attending the SJT, parties with settlement authority try to reach an agreement. If settlement is not reached, the parties are still entitled to a full trial in court.

The SJT was developed by Judge Thomas Lambros of the United States District Court for the Northern District of Ohio in an effort to alleviate overcrowded dockets in the civil justice system. Judge Lambros theorized that disputing parties would be more willing to settle cases and forego trials if they had a reasonable prediction of what a jury would do in their case. He relied on Rule 16 FRCP (Appendix) for authority to convene the SJT.

The SJT is certainly not without its critics. Some have objected to courts requiring parties to use the process; some courts do so. Others object to using public courthouse facilities for private settlement purposes. It has been endorsed, however, by the Judicial Conference of the United States and the Civil Justice Reform Act of 1990. Numerous federal and state courts have reported success with the process.

2. Governing Principles

Traditional settlement discussions often fail when the parties' perceptions of the merits of a case are significantly different from those of their adversary. Differing views of the merits of a case result from a number of factors. Lawyers may assess a potential outcome on a key issue erroneously. The parties may have an unrealistic assessment of what the potential outcome will be at trial, where they have an exaggerated sense of the worth of their case. This may result from poor client counseling on the part of their lawyers or from their own expectations. For example, the severely injured victim in a product liability case would not be willing to settle for one million dollars if he thinks that a jury will award him three million dollars. After learning that SJT jurors had awarded him $500,000.00 in damages following the SJT, the injured victim and his lawyer might be more inclined to settle the case for one million dollars.

The SJT is useful for cases which will probably not settle in traditional settlement negotiations where parties usually rely on the lawyers' or judge's sense of case evaluation. Based on prior experience, each side and the judge come up with a set of numbers. When this occurs, the parties cannot come to a meeting of the minds because of differing expectations about the value of a case. The SJT acts as the agent of reality and the tie-breaker. On the other hand, the SJT may not be advisable where the credibility of a witness is the critical issue in the case. Given the inherent time constraints of the process, it is generally not possible to subject witnesses to the full examination of trial. But parties have employed live witness testimony and cross examination in SJT's when necessary to resolve a factual issue. Finally, where a question of law is unsettled and needs to be resolved by a court, the SJT is usually not appropriate.

3. The Summary Jury Trial Process

The SJT usually takes place after discovery has been substantially completed and pending motions have been resolved. Where parties target their discovery toward critical or key issues focused on settlement, the SJT can be conducted at an earlier time while reserving complex discovery for any trial that may occur. Because it is designed to be a flexible device, procedures vary in different courts. Under the Lambros model, the trial is conducted in a courtroom with either a judge or magistrate presiding. Lawyers for each side submit a trial brief on the issues of law as well as proposed jury instructions.

A six member advisory jury is selected from the regular jury panel through an abbreviated voir dire examination. Each side is allowed two peremptory challenges. In most cases the jurors are not told that their verdict is nonbinding until the SJT is completed. Clients are required to attend the trial and corporate clients must be represented by an agent with settlement authority.

Lawyers make opening statements and then make summary presentations of their cases. The summarizations must be based on admissible evidence. Formal objections are discouraged. Some courts have allowed live witness testimony. Following rebuttal and closing arguments by counsel, the court charges the jury on the law and the jury then renders a consensus verdict. If jurors are unable to reach consensus, they may return individual verdicts describing each juror's opinion on liability and damages.

Post-trial proceedings begin with a debriefing session in which counsel for both parties have an opportunity to question the jurors after the verdict is rendered. This session gives the parties valuable insight on the individual juror's reaction to their cases. What evidence worked? Which arguments fell flat? Which facts were deemed weak? What swayed the jurors? The parties with settlement authority then meet privately to conduct settlement discussions in light of the jury's verdict. Regardless of the outcome of the SJT, the parties retain the right to a full trial on the merits.

The total hearing usually lasts for one day but it may be longer. Parties who use the SJT generally seek the same degree of confidentiality that settlement negotiations enjoy. The proceedings generally are not recorded. No statements, communications or jury findings from the SJT are admissible at a later trial on the merits.

4. Major Advantages of the Summary Jury Trial

The SJT simulates an actual trial from voir dire to jury instruction thereby giving parties who want their day in court a taste of the real thing without the risks and costs of a full blown trial. The major advantages of the SJT are the predictive feature of the advisory jury verdict combined with the wide range of settlement possibilities that parties can pursue in the negotiation phase without being bound by any decision of a jury. When the parties have advance notice of what a jury is likely to do, they have a more reasonable understanding of the parameters of the settlement range. Clients have a realistic incentive to settle because they have learned first-hand from watching the SJT the strengths and weaknesses of their case.

Another advantage of the SJT is the savings in time and money which would have been spent on a full trial. Attorneys' fees are considerably reduced because the proceeding is short. Even if the SJT does not result in settlement, the lawyers' time and effort in preparing for the SJT has not been wasted. The parties have organized their cases, the issues have been refined and the resulting trial should be a more efficient process.

The SJT also benefits the courts by providing new case management options in appropriate situations. Every case does not have to run the full nine yards for the litigants to experience a just resolution of their cases. Anecdotal reports show a great time savings to the courts. For example, in *McKay v. Ashland Oil, Inc.* (1988), the court wrote: "In my own experience summary jury trials have netted me a savings in time of about 60 days and I have only used the procedure five times. It settled two of these cases that were set for 30–day trials." Judge Lambros reports that he has used the procedure successfully in over 1,000 mass toxic tort cases. In general, reports show that the SJT has been used successfully in a wide range of actions including: negligence, products liability, toxic tort, personal injury, contract, discrimination, admiralty and antitrust. Certainly there is room for more empirical studies of the SJT before a final assessment of its value can be made.

5. Criticisms of the Summary Jury Trial

Some judges and lawyers have raised several concerns about the value of SJTs. First, some critics argue that because lawyers make the major case presentations, there is no cross-examination of witnesses, and therefore, the SJT fails to assess the credibility of witnesses. Unless credibility is the central issue however, parties can test credibility through the use of documentary evidence and abbreviated cross-examination. A second criticism argues that the transaction costs of preparing for the SJT may actually increase the cost of litigation if the process does not result in settlement. Such preparation, however, can also reduce the costs of the eventual trial. Finally, there are concerns with protecting confidentiality. Critics argue that compelling parties to participate in the SJT may result in disclosure of privileged information. While some courts do compel use, others require voluntary agreements if the process is employed. Moreover, the evidence is subject to court admissibility standards.

6. Case Law Development

(i) Power to Compel Parties to Participate

The SJT has spurned considerable cases and commentary related to the legal power of a federal court to order parties to participate in the process. Supporters of the SJT believe that the authority for requiring parties to participate in SJTs derives from two sources: the inherent power of the court to manage its calendar and the pre-trial powers of a court pursuant to Rule 16 of the Federal Rules of Civil Procedure. (Appendix) Rule 16 gives judges substantial pre-trial authority but it does not expressly empower federal courts to order SJTs.

Most courts which have considered the compulsion issue, have held, however, that mandating participation in a SJT is a permissible exercise of judicial power, e.g., *McKay v. Ashland Oil, Inc.* (1988). A few courts, notably, *Strandell v. Jackson County* (1987), have held that no such power exists.

Strandall involved a criminal contempt charge against an attorney who represented a civil rights plaintiff. The attorney refused to participate in a SJT after being ordered to do so by the court because he believed that it required him to reveal privileged information. This would result in giving his opponents an unfair advantage. The Seventh Circuit Court of Appeals vacated his contempt judgment holding that the pre-trial conference of Rule 16 was intended simply to generate settlement discussions and not "to require that an unwilling litigant be sidetracked from the normal course of litigation."

(ii) Right of Access

Use of the SJT has also raised First Amendment questions, specifically, whether the right of press access into the courtroom attaches to the SJT. In *Cincinnati Gas & Electric Co. v. General Electric Co.* (1988) the Sixth Circuit Court of Appeals held that the First Amendment right of access does not apply to the SJT on the theory that the "summary jury trial does not present any matter for adjudication by the court." The court also observed that the SJT is similar to a settlement discussion which historically has been considered a private proceeding and concluded that public access to this proceeding would not add anything to its effectiveness.

(iii) Authority of the Court to Empanel the Advisory Jury

A court's authority to empanel advisory jurors was sharply questioned in *Hume v. M & C Management* (1990) wherein a federal district court judge wrote that courts "... have no authority to summon citizens to serve as settlement advisors, just as they would have no authority to summon citizens to serve as hand servants for themselves, lawyers or litigants."

Both parties in *Hume* asked the court to convene a SJT according to the Lambros model following unsuccessful settlement discussions in a Fair Housing case. The court denied the motion on the grounds that federal judges lacked authority to require citizens to serve as jurors in the SJT. The court based its holding on a provision in the Jury Selection and Service Act of 1968 that requires citizens to serve only on "grand" and "petit" juries. In a footnote reference to Judge Posner's criticisms of the SJT, the court noted that SJT's could compromise the integrity of the jury system.

Even though there is no specific statutory authority for using persons as summary jurors, the court may well have the power to do so through its inherent power to manage its docket.

II. EARLY NEUTRAL EVALUATION

1. Overview

Early Neutral Evaluation (ENE) is a relatively new form of judicial, court-annexed ADR which involves early, systematic case assessment by a private attorney experienced in the substantive area of the dispute. The objective analysis by a neutral evaluator forces attorneys and their clients to confront their own and their opponent's case at an early juncture in the litigation process before adversarial pre-trial battles blind them to opportunities for settlement.

The first ENE program began on an experimental basis in the Northern District of California in 1985. As a result of the program's success, it became a permanent feature of that court in 1988. ENE programs have now expanded to other federal districts and seem to be enthusiastically supported by the judges who work with them.

2. How ENE Operates

An ENE procedure based on the Northern District of California model operates generally in the following manner. After the first status conference, parties are required to attend a confidential evaluation session directed by a court-appointed lawyer who is experienced in the substantive area of the dispute. At least seven days before the evaluation session, the parties must submit written statements identifying significant issues, the type of discovery which would be helpful in shaping settlement and the names of any representatives of the opposing party whose presence would assist in settlement. The court orders the client to attend the evaluation session.

A typical session begins with an opening statement by the neutral evaluator. The parties then present a narrative of their case and exchange detailed information. The rules of evidence do not apply and there is no formal examination or cross-examination of witnesses. All communications at the evaluation session are protected from disclosure.

Following the parties' case presentation, the neutral offers assistance in a number of ways: by helping the parties identify their areas of agreement and entering into stipulations where appropriate; by assessing the strengths and weakness of the parties' arguments and evidence; by estimating, where feasible, the likelihood of liability and the dollar range of damages as a spur to settlement; and by helping the parties make a plan for conducting discovery. It may well be, however, that the parties are willing to share more information after the presentations and therefore, extensive discovery will not be necessary. The evaluator may also assist in mediating settlement discussions arising from the evaluation.

3. On The Merits

ENE bears some resemblance to the mini-trial and the judicial status conference but there are definite differences. Compared to the mini-trial, ENE is a less complicated procedure. The parties and their lawyers are required to attend the evaluation session and the neutral evaluator is chosen by the court, not the parties. Proponents of ENE suggest that it is more productive than the typical judicial status conference because the neutral evaluator is not bound by the ethical and time constraints imposed upon judges and can therefore probe more deeply into the dispute than judges are able to do. Discussions are more focused and the parties therefore have a better understanding of the parameters of the dispute.

The key to successful use of ENE as with all ADR processes, lies in identification of the appropriate cases. Experience thus far suggests that the type of cases that can benefit from ENE are commercial contract and tort cases where there are obvious, clear-cut differences between the parties regarding the valuation of the case. In some situations, ENE may be appropriate for only some issues such as differences over the amount of damages, while other issues may more suited for mediation, arbitration or litigation.

III. MAGISTRATES, SPECIAL MASTERS, AND NEUTRAL EXPERTS

The growth of multi-party, complex litigation such as the asbestos, Dalkon Shield and Agent Orange cases, has strained judicial resources and forced the civil justice system to develop new and more efficient methods of case management. Towards this end, the courts have made increased use of magistrates, special masters, and neutral experts to assist with settlement efforts and to develop claims facilities in mass tort and other complex cases. The individuals appointed in these cases are usually either retired judges, lawyers with technical expertise or lawyers with specialized knowledge in a substantive area such as environmental law or toxic torts. As judicial adjuncts, they are not constrained by the limitations imposed on Article III judges. Theoretically, they have more time to spend on managing cases and are therefore more accessible to the litigants. They are also more free to explore settlement techniques than the assigned judges who may have to try the case if settlement attempts fail and, therefore, cannot get deeply embroiled in mediation attempts.

Of course, there can be some negative results with the use of this judicial support system if the masters, magistrates and experts are not selected carefully. Ineffective masters and magistrates, for example, could prolong the discovery process, increase motion practice and undermine confidence in the judicial system.

1. Magistrates

Federal magistrates are appointed by the court pursuant to the Federal Magistrates Act, 28 U.S.C.A. § 631 et seq. which was enacted in 1968. In accordance with the Act, judges from each district may appoint magistrates to perform specified statutory functions and "additional duties as are not inconsistent with the Constitution and laws of the United States." One example of appropriate "additional duties" for a magistrate is described in *Mathews v. Weber* (1976), an action challenging a district court rule that referred all social security appeals to a magistrate for initial review. The rule directed the magistrate to conduct hearings and prepare a written proposed order with proposed findings of fact and conclusions of law. The Supreme Court held that the preliminary review assignment given to the magistrate in this case was one of the "additional duties" contemplated by the Act.

Magistrates aid district court judges in a variety of ways including conducting discovery in mass tort cases, conducting Early Neutral Evaluation (ENE) conferences and hosting judicial settlement conferences. There is a growing tendency to assign even greater case management and settlement responsibilities to magistrates as federal district courts study their caseloads and begin to develop "civil justice expense and delay reduction plan[s]" (EDRP's) in response to the Civil Justice Reform Act of 1990.

2. Masters

Courts have inherent authority as well as authority under Rule 53 of the Federal Rules of Civil Procedure to appoint special masters. Rule 53 provides in relevant part:

Rule 53. Masters

(c) *Powers.* The order of reference to the master may specify or limit the master's powers and may direct the master to report only upon particular issues or to do or perform particular acts or to receive and report evidence only .... Subject to the specifications and limitations stated in the order, the master has and shall exercise the power to regulate all proceedings in every hearing before the master and to do all acts and take all measures necessary or proper for the efficient performance of the master's duties under the order ....

The court may appoint a special master when exceptional conditions are present in a case or because the complexity of litigation requires additional assistance. For example, in *United States v. Suquamish Indian Tribe* (1990), the Ninth Circuit Court of Appeals upheld the referral to a special master the issue of determining whether the Suquamish Indian tribe could assert the fishing rights of another tribe as a successor in interest.

It is useful if the litigants and judge agree on the appointment of a specific person as a master. Where the litigants have confidence and trust in the master's ability to manage a case and facilitate settlement, there is a greater opportunity for a collaborative effort to settle the case.

The traditional role of masters has largely been ministerial and adjudicatory, i.e., render accountings, preside over hearings and make findings of fact and recommendations. More recently, however, masters are functioning as facilitators in the settlement of complex disputes. One model, adopted by Judge Marvin Aspen of the Northern District of Illinois, uses special masters as mediators. Special master mediation has proved to be successful in complex disputes under the following conditions: where traditional settlement attempts have failed; where sufficient discovery has been completed so that both sides are educated about the case; and, where the parties are willing to participate in the mediation process.

Another special master model which has been used successfully in the Northern District of California, uses prominent attorneys to serve as settlement masters. Under this approach, the master examines cases filed on the civil docket on a regular basis and seeks cases for settlement where the subject matter of the dispute is within the legal expertise of the master. Assuming that the parties have an interest in settlement and that they can afford the master's fee, the court refers the case to the settlement master.

One of the most publicized uses of a special master as settlement facilitator involved a complex dispute over fishing rights in the Great Lakes. *United States v. Michigan* (1979). This case had a twelve year litigation history and numerous parties including several tribes of Indians and various federal government officials. The parties all had deeply held political beliefs that seemed to resist compromise.

Judge Richard A. Enslen appointed a law professor, Frances McGovern, as a special master in the case and authorized him to oversee pre-trial developments and to conduct settlement discussions. The judge was insulated from any of the details of the settlement discussions. Professor McGovern writes that the case presented a classic example of polycentric issues which could not be easily resolved in an adjudication process:

The solution to any given question concerning resource division was dependent upon the solutions reached on the other questions: no issues were independent. This complex interrelationship of issues created difficulties which were compounded by the lack of any—much less clear—legal standards. The court was being asked to make extremely complex management decisions by using policy differences unreflected in the substantive law—"reasonable living standards," "subsistence," "maximizing value," and "equal distribution."

McGovern, *"Toward A Functional Approach for Managing Complex Litigation,"* 53 U.Chi.L.Rev. 440, 459 (1986).

After establishing an abbreviated discovery schedule, the master focused on facilitating a settlement. Using a computer-assisted negotiation model, the master helped the parties arrive at an agreement after only three days of negotiations. Only one tribe refused to be bound by the agreement and proceeded with litigation.

3. Neutral Experts

Neutral fact-finding is an informal process in which a neutral third party studies a particular issue and reports findings on that issue. The court may appoint neutral experts in accordance with Rule 706 of the Federal Rules of Evidence which provides in part:

Rule 706. Court Appointed Experts

(a) *Appointment.* The court may on its own motion or on the motion of any party enter an order to show cause why expert witnesses should not be appointed, and may request the parties to submit nominations. The court may appoint any expert witnesses agreed upon by the parties, and may appoint expert witnesses of its own selection .... A witness so appointed shall advise the parties of the witness' findings, if any;

the witness' deposition may be taken by any party; and the witness may be called to testify by the court or any party. The witness shall be subject to cross-examination by each party, including a party calling the witness.

The courts enjoy broad discretion in deciding whether to appoint a neutral witness and individual parties cannot require that the court do so. Generally, a judge would wait until discovery has been substantially developed before determining the need for an expert. In cases involving complex technical or scientific issues, use of a neutral expert may be the most efficient means of resolving a dispute.

The conclusions of the expert witness may take the form of an oral or written report to the court or to the parties. Alternatively, the expert may be required to testify and be subject to cross-examination.

Just as magistrates and masters are assuming increased importance in settlement negotiations, so too are court-appointed experts. Because of their technical expertise in areas such as patent infringement, copyright, trade secret violations, antitrust cases, these experts bring greater understanding to the substantive aspects of complex disputes and are often better able to fashion creative solutions than are judges.

BIBLIOGRAPHY

Brazil, *"Early Neutral Evaluation,"* from *A Close Look at Three Court–Sponsored ADR Programs,* 1990 U.Chi.Legal F. 303.

Brazil, *"Special Masters in Complex Cases: Extending the Judiciary or Reshaping Adjudication,"* 53 U.Chi.L.Rev. 394 (1986);

Brazil, *"Judicial Adjuncts: Special Masters and Court–Appointed Experts,"* Chapter 5 in *ADR and the Courts: A Manual for Judges and Lawyers, CPR Legal Program* (Butterworth Publications 1987);

Lambros, *"The Summary Jury Trial and Other Alternative Methods of Dispute Resolution: A Report to the Judicial Conference of the United States, Committee on the Operation of the Jury System,"* 103 F.R.D. 461 (1984).

Levine, *"Northern District of California Adopts Early Neutral Evaluation to Expedite Dispute Resolution,"* 72 Judicature 235 (1989).

McGovern, *"Toward A Functional Approach for Managing Complex Litigation,"* 53 U.Chi.L.Rev. 440 (1986).

Posner, *"The Summary Jury Trial and Other Methods of Alternative Dispute Resolution: Some Cautionary Observations,"* 53 U.Chi.L.Rev. 366 (1986).

Wiegand, *"A New Light Bulb or the Work of the Devil? A Current Assessment of Summary Jury Trial,"* 69 Or.L.Rev. 87 (1990).

CHAPTER 6

HYBRID DISPUTE RESOLUTION PROCEDURES

The continued growth of the ADR movement has resulted in several innovative combinations of dispute resolution processes. Facilitated negotiation can combine with mediation in the mini-trial. It blends with regulatory rule-making in the "neg-reg" process. Mediation connects with arbitration in the "med-arb" process. Two other processes, reference and ombuds procedures, while not new, are being used with much more frequency today than in the past. Private adjudication comprises the essence of reference or "rent-a-judge" procedures. Finally, the role of ombudsperson involves mediation and fact-finding.

I. THE MINI–TRIAL

1. Definition

The mini-trial is not really a trial in any meaningful sense of that word. Rather, it is a structured settlement process which can blend together some components of negotiation, mediation and adversarial case presentation. A mutually agreeable neutral advisor usually presides over the proceeding. It has two phases: first, counsel for each side make abbreviated but adversarial presentations of their "best" cases to senior management executives with full settlement authority. Then, following the hearing, the business executives discuss settlement. The process is private and voluntary.

The phrase "mini-trial" was coined by a New York Times journalist in 1977 to describe successful settlement negotiations in a complex patent infringement case between TRW Inc. and Telecredit, Inc. involving millions of dollars. The hypnotic power of those words have attached to this process ever since that time.

2. The Structure of a Mini–Trial

The mini-trial is a flexible procedure which may be tailored to meet individual litigant needs, therefore, the format for individual hearings varies. In general, parties would initiate the mini-trial by entering into an agreement describing the procedures which would govern the process. A typical agreement would include provisions for conducting discovery, selection of the neutral adviser, exchange of position papers, the individuals from each organization who will serve on the mini-trial panel and confidentiality provisions. Sample procedures for a mini-trial appear at the end of this section.

There are essentially three structural phases of the minitrial: a discovery phase; the actual hearing and post-hearing settlement discussions by the parties.

Discovery is usually brief but it must be sufficient for each side to appreciate the key issues involved in the case. At a minimum, the parties would exchange key exhibits, introductory statements and a summary of witnesses' testimony.

At the hearing which is also referred to as the "information exchange," counsel for each party make summary presentations of their cases to senior management representatives. The legal and factual issues have been distilled by this time so that these presentations are able to focus on the underlying merits of the dispute. It is important that the management representatives have settlement authority. Otherwise, the full impact of the face-to-face presentations is diluted.

The hearing is intended to be informal and the rules of evidence and civil procedure are typically waived but it is structured around adversarial presentation and rebuttal of positions. The confidentiality of the procedure encourages free and open discussion. The neutral advisor, usually an attorney or retired judge, may comment on the arguments or evidence, and question the witnesses or counsel. Hearing this commentary and questioning helps the executives hearing the case to appreciate the strength and weaknesses of their own cases and the opponents' cases. Following the information exchange between counsel, the parties may request that the neutral advisor evaluate the

case and offer an opinion as to the probable outcome if the case were tried in court. The neutral's
opinion can have a significant impact on the parties decision to settle, particularly where the neutral is a retired judge or a seasoned trial attorney
with experience in the type of case involved in the
dispute. The neutral may also be asked to mediate
during the settlement discussions.

In some situations, the parties may decide not to
use a neutral advisor to conduct the information
exchange. Following the hearing, the parties
would simply attempt to negotiate a settlement on
their own with the assistance of their attorneys.

3. The Settlement Discussions

Senior management representatives who have
attended the information exchange enter into post-
hearing negotiation discussions with a view towards reaching an out-of-court settlement. While
the mini-trial usually takes one day, it may take a
few weeks to reach an agreement.

Settlement discussions following a mini-trial differ from traditional negotiation in a number of
respects. First, the discussions are more focused
after a mini-trial. The summary presentations by
counsel have cut away the "fat" and honed in on
the critical issues in dispute. The parties have a
much better sense of the strengths and weaknesses
of their cases. More realistic dialogue is possible
because discussion is not between the initial par-

ties to the dispute or the lawyers who continued to press the dispute, but between high level executive personnel who, theoretically, are removed from the emotional aspects of disputing.

If the parties are still unable to settle the case on their own during the post-hearing settlement talks, they may agree that the neutral advisor will act as a mediator. Even if the case does not settle, the mini-trial is still considered an efficient process because the time spent in preparing for the information exchange helps organize the courtroom trial.

4. Appropriate Use of the Mini-trial

The mini-trial has proved to be successful in complex civil cases where there are mixed questions of law and fact. It has been used successfully in cases involving patent infringement, government contracts, products liability, antitrust, construction and contract enforcement. On the other hand, there are inherent limitations to this process. Where one of the parties needs the cathartic effect of trial, the short-hand version of a trial will probably prove unsatisfactory. If one of the parties has no serious desire to settle, the mini-trial is probably a waste of time. The following guidelines are representative of the procedures which would be used at a mini-trial administered by the American Arbitration Association. Guidelines for non-administered mini-trial procedures

are available from the Center for Public Resources
in New York City.

AMERICAN ARBITRATION ASSOCIATION
MINI–TRIAL PROCEDURES

1. The mini-trial process may be initiated by
the written or oral request of either party, made to
any regional office of the AAA, but will not be
pursued unless both parties agree to resolve their
dispute by means of a mini-trial.

2. The course of the mini-trial process shall be
governed by a written agreement between the parties.

3. The mini-trial shall consist of an information
exchange and settlement negotiation.

4. Each party is represented throughout the
mini-trial process by legal counsel whose role is to
prepare and present the party's "best case" at the
information exchange.

5. Each party shall have in attendance
throughout the information exchange and settlement negotiation a senior executive with settlement authority.

6. A neutral advisor shall be present at the
information exchange to decide questions of procedure and to render advice to the party representatives when requested by them.

7. The neutral advisor shall be selected by mutual agreement of the parties, who may consult
with the AAA for recommendations. To facilitate

the selection process, the AAA will make available to the parties a list of individuals to serve as neutral advisors. If the parties fail to agree upon the selection of a neutral advisor, they shall ask that the AAA appoint an advisor from the panel it has compiled for this purpose.

8. Discovery between the parties may take place prior to the information exchange, in accordance with the agreement between the parties.

9. Prior to the information exchange, the parties shall exchange written statements summarizing the issues in the case, and copies of all documents they intend to present at the information exchange.

10. Federal or state rules of evidence do not apply to presentations made at the information exchange. Any limitation on the scope of the evidence offered at the information exchange shall be determined by mutual agreement of the parties prior to the exchange and shall be enforced by the neutral advisor.

11. After the information exchange, the senior executives shall meet and attempt, in good faith, to formulate a voluntary settlement of the dispute.

12. If the senior executives are unable to settle the dispute, the neutral advisor shall render an advisory opinion as to the likely outcome of the case if it were litigated in a court of law. The neutral advisor's opinion shall identify the issues of law and fact which are critical to the disposition

of the case and give the reasons for the opinion that is offered.

13. After the neutral advisor has rendered an advisory opinion, the senior executives shall meet for a second time in an attempt to resolve the dispute. If they are unable to reach a settlement at this time, they may either abandon the proceeding or submit to the neutral advisor written offers of settlement. If the parties elect to make such written offers, the neutral advisor shall make a recommendation for settlement based on those offers. If the parties reject the recommendation of the neutral advisor, either party may declare the mini-trial terminated and resolve the dispute by other means.

14. Mini-trial proceedings are confidential; no written or oral statement made by any participant in the proceeding may be used as evidence or in admission in any other proceeding.

15. The fees and expenses of the neutral advisor shall be borne equally by the parties, and each party is responsible for its own costs, including legal fees, incurred in connection with the mini-trial. The parties may, however, in their written agreement alter the allocation of fees and expenses.

16. Neither the AAA nor any neutral advisor serving in a mini-trial proceeding governed by these procedures shall be liable to any party for any act or omission in connection with the mini-trial. The parties shall indemnify the AAA and

the neutral advisor for any liability to third parties arising out of the mini-trial process.

Mini–Trial Fee Schedule

Administrative Fee

Parties initiating a mini-trial under these procedures will make arrangements with the AAA regional office for administrative fees and neutral advisor compensation.

II. REFERENCE PROCEDURES

Almost every state permits cases to be referred to private judges whose authority is equivalent to that of the public judiciary. Reference procedures, also known as "private judging" or "rent-a-judge," vary in each state in the amount of power given to the referee, the effect of the referee's decision, the amount of public involvement in the process and the extent to which it has the force of public adjudication. The litigants select and pay for the referee who is often a retired judge. In some states the decision of the referee has the force and effect of a trial court judgment.

The major benefit of using a reference procedure is speed. In by-passing the traditional court structure, litigants avoid the systemic weaknesses of the judicial system, specifically, the long wait for a day in court. Other advantages of reference procedures over public judging are privacy and the ability to select the referee. Unlike the arbitration process to which it bears similarities, litigants have the right of full review of the referee's decision.

Reference systems have been criticized on public policy grounds for their lack of public accountability and for creating a two-tiered system of justice where the wealthy who can afford to, use personally selected private judges and the poor are relegated to the public system of justice. Private judging has also been criticized for luring talented public judges off the bench to the private sector where they earn high hourly rates for judging. However, the full due process system available in the regular courts to any litigant, weakens this criticism.

III. MED–ARB

In the traditional med-arb process, the same person serves as both a mediator and an arbitrator in one dispute. In effect, the third party neutral functions as a catalyst for the settlement process because the presence of the neutral who may ultimately have to make a decision in the case gives the parties a realistic incentive to settle. The med-arb process originated in the collective bargaining context where it has been referred to as "muscle" mediation. Today, the med-arb process has been adopted in some commercial cases and in court-annexed programs.

Med-arb is considered a more efficient process than straight mediation followed by arbitration with a different person—if the mediation process does not result in an agreement, it will not be necessary for the parties to begin their story all over again with a new arbitrator. On the other hand, the med-arb process has been criticized on the grounds that it may be difficult, if not impossible for the person who learned confidential information as a mediator to render an objective decision as an arbitrator. For example, assume that a neutral learns in a private mediation caucus that the plaintiff in a $100,000.00 products liability case is really willing to settle the case for $35,000.00 (even though the case is worth at least $65,000.00.) If the case does not settle in mediation and the same neutral awards $35,000.00 to the plaintiff in arbitration, there are serious concerns about the fairness of that award.

In some variations of the med-arb process, the mediator acts simply as an advisory arbitrator. When the parties are informed as to what the arbitrator's decision would be, they may be induced to settle on their own. In other models, the mediator recommends to the court how the dispute should be resolved. In California, for example, a statute mandating mediation permits a mediator to make recommendations to the court regarding child custody and visitation issues.

IV. NEGOTIATED RULEMAKING

Growing discontent with the delays and court challenges attached to the traditional federal rulemaking process led regulatory reformers to propose negotiation as a preferred method of rulemaking. The concept of negotiated rulemaking, also known as "neg-reg," or regulatory negotiation, involves direct participation in rulemaking by public agency regulators and the private business and advocacy groups affected by the regulations. The goal of the process is to reach consensus.

Negotiated rulemaking avoids the adversarial approach of traditional notice and comment rulemaking where a final draft of a regulation is given to affected parties for comment. Special interest concerns would invariably cause many regulations to be challenged and time-consuming court battles would be initiated. Face-to-face negotiations at the initial drafting stages promotes a problem-solving approach which is likely to leave the affected parties more satisfied with the result.

Advocates of negotiated rulemaking refer to its potential to make rules more acceptable to affected parties and thus less likely to be challenged in court. By direct participation and collaborative efforts, the affected parties invest in the rulemaking process and therefore, claim some ownership of the substantive result.

Negotiated rulemaking has been used successfully by a number of federal agencies and the benefits of the process were officially recognized in The Negotiated Rulemaking Act of 1990, an amendment to the Administrative Procedure Act. Section 2 of the Act reflects Congress' findings that negotiated rulemaking can provide significant advantages over current adversarial rulemaking procedures which "may discourage the affected parties from meeting and communicating with each other, and may cause parties with different interests to assume conflicting and antagonistic positions and to engage in expensive and time-consuming litigation over agency rules."

On the other hand, "negotiated rulemaking can increase the acceptability and improve the substance of rules, making it less likely that the affected parties will resist enforcement or challenge such rules in court."

Under the scheme established in the Act, a federal agency may establish a negotiated rulemaking committee if the head of the agency determines that such a procedure would be in the public interest. The statute lists several factors which would go into this determination including need, adequate resources and reasonable likelihood that there could be a committee with balanced representation of persons. If the agency does decide to convene a committee, notice of this intent must be published in the Federal Register and appropriate trade magazines.

After considering comments, the agency may or may not decide to establish a negotiated rulemaking committee. The committee terminates upon the promulgation of the final rule under consideration.

V. OMBUDSPERSON

An ombudsperson is a neutral individual who hears complaints, engages in fact finding, and generally promotes the resolution of disputes through informal methods such as mediation and counseling. An ombudsperson may also be referred to as an ombuds or ombudsman.

The traditional notion of an "ombudsman" derives from the Scandanavian countries where a public official would be designated to listen to the public's complaints and attempt to respond to them. In the United States, however, ombudspersons are often employed by private organizations to act as in-house neutrals in responding to employment-related problems. In many corporations, hospitals and universities for example, the office of ombudsperson functions as an official "complaint department" with clout. Employees can engage in the venting process and be assured of confidentiality, respect and fair dealing. The ombudsperson may be able to make constructive recommendations for change to management without even revealing the identity of the complaining employee.

BIBLIOGRAPHY

Lon Fuller, "*Collective Bargaining and the Arbitrator*," Proceedings, Fifteenth Annual Meeting, National Academy of Arbitrators, Washington, D.C.: Bureau of National Affairs (1962);

Stephen Goldberg, *The Mediation of Grievances Under a Collective Bargaining Contract: An Alternative to Arbitration,* 77 Nw.U.L.Rev. 270 (1982).

Harter, *"Negotiating Regulations: A Cure for Malaise,"* 71 Geo.L.J. 1, 6 (1982).

Note, *"The California Rent–A–Judge Experiment: Constitutional and Policy Considerations of Pay As You Go Courts,"* 94 Harv.L.Rev. 1592 (1981).

Mary P. Rowe, *"The Ombudsman's Role in a Dispute Resolution System,"* 7 Neg.J. 353 (1991).

APPENDIX A

FEDERAL RULES OF EVIDENCE—RULE 408

COMPROMISE AND OFFERS TO COMPROMISE

Evidence of (1) furnishing or offering or promising to furnish, or (2) accepting or offering or promising to accept, a valuable consideration in compromising or attempting to compromise a claim which was disputed as to either validity or amount, is not admissible to prove liability for or invalidity of the claim or its amount. Evidence of conduct or statements made in compromise negotiations is likewise not admissible. This rule does not require the exclusion of any evidence otherwise discoverable merely because it is presented in the course of compromise negotiations. This rule also does not require exclusion when the evidence is offered for another purpose, such as proving bias or prejudice of a witness, negativing a contention of undue delay, or proving an effort to obstruct a criminal investigation or prosecution.

APPENDIX B

FEDERAL RULES OF CIVIL PROCEDURE—RULE 16

PRETRIAL CONFERENCE; SCHEDULING; MANAGEMENT

(a) **Pretrial Conferences; Objectives.** In any action, the court may in its discretion direct the attorneys for the parties and any unrepresented parties to appear before it for a conference or conferences before trial for such purposes as

(1) expediting the disposition of the action;

(2) establishing early and continuing control so that the case will not be protracted because of lack of management;

(3) discouraging wasteful pretrial activities;

(4) improving the quality of the trial through more thorough preparation, and;

(5) facilitating the settlement of the case.

(b) **Scheduling and Planning.** Except in categories of actions exempted by district court rule as inappropriate, the judge, or a magistrate when authorized by district court rule, shall, after consulting with the attorneys for the parties and any unrepresented parties, by a scheduling conference,

telephone, mail, or other suitable means, enter a
scheduling order that limits the time

(1) to join other parties and to amend the
pleadings;

(2) to file and hear motions;

(3) to complete discovery.

The scheduling order also may include

(4) the date or dates for conferences before
trial, a final pretrial conference, and trial; and

(5) any other matters appropriate in the circumstances of the case.

The order shall issue as soon as practicable but in
no event more than 120 days after filing of the
complaint. A schedule shall not be modified except by leave of the judge or a magistrate when
authorized by district court rule upon a showing of
good cause.

(c) **Subjects to Be Discussed at Pretrial Conferences.** The participants at any conference under this rule may consider and take action with
respect to

(1) the formulation and simplification of the
issues, including the elimination of frivolous
claims or defenses;

(2) the necessity or desirability of amendments
to the pleadings;

(3) the possibility of obtaining admissions of
fact and of documents which will avoid unnecessary proof, stipulations regarding the authentici-

ty of documents, and advance rulings from the court on the admissibility of evidence;

(4) the avoidance of unnecessary proof and of cumulative evidence;

(5) the identification of witnesses and documents, the need and schedule for filing and exchanging pretrial briefs, and the date or dates for further conferences and for trial;

(6) the advisability of referring matters to a magistrate or master;

(7) the possibility of settlement or the use of extrajudicial procedures to resolve the dispute;

(8) the form and substance of the pretrial order;

(9) the disposition of pending motions;

(10) the need for adopting special procedures for managing potentially difficult or protracted actions that may involve complex issues, multiple parties, difficult legal questions, or unusual proof problems; and

(11) such other matters as may aid in the disposition of the action.

At least one of the attorneys for each party participating in any conference before trial shall have authority to enter into stipulations and to make admissions regarding all matters that the participants may reasonably anticipate may be discussed.

(d) **Final Pretrial Conference.** Any final pretrial conference shall be held as close to the time of trial as reasonable under the circumstances. The participants at any such conference shall formulate a plan for trial, including a program for facilitating the admission of evidence. The conference shall be attended by at least one of the attorneys who will conduct the trial for each of the parties and by any unrepresented parties.

(e) **Pretrial Orders.** After any conference held pursuant to this rule, an order shall be entered reciting the action taken. This order shall control the subsequent course of the action unless modified by a subsequent order. The order following a final pretrial conference shall be modified only to prevent manifest injustice.

(f) **Sanctions.** If a party or party's attorney fails to obey a scheduling or pretrial order, or if no appearance is made on behalf of a party at a scheduling or pretrial conference, or if a party or party's attorney is substantially unprepared to participate in the conference, or if a party or party's attorney fails to participate in good faith, the judge, upon motion or the judge's own initiative, may make such orders with regard thereto as are just, and among others any of the orders provided in Rule 37(b)(2)(B), (C), (D).* In lieu of or in addi-

* ["(B) An order refusing to allow the disobedient party to support or oppose designated claims or defenses, or prohibiting that party from introducing designated matters in evidence; (C) An order striking out pleadings or parts thereof, or staying further proceedings until the order is obeyed, or dismissing the action or proceeding or any part thereof, or rendering a judgment by default against the disobedient party; (D) In lieu of any of the foregoing orders or in addition thereto, an order treating as a contempt of court the failure to obey any orders except an

tion to any other sanction, the judge shall require the party or the attorney representing the party or both to pay the reasonable expenses incurred because of any noncompliance with this rule, including attorney's fees, unless the judge finds that the noncompliance was substantially justified or that other circumstances make an award of expenses unjust.

As amended 1983, 1987.

order to submit to a physical or mental examination." Rule 37(b)(2).]

APPENDIX C

FEDERAL RULES OF CIVIL PROCEDURE—RULE 68

OFFER OF JUDGMENT

At any time more than 10 days before the trial begins, a party defending against a claim may serve upon the adverse party an offer to allow judgment to be taken against the defending party for the money or property or to the effect specified in the offer, with costs then accrued. If within 10 days after the service of the offer the adverse party serves written notice that the offer is accepted, either party may then file the offer and notice of acceptance together with proof of service thereof and thereupon the clerk shall enter judgment. An offer not accepted shall be deemed withdrawn and evidence thereof is not admissible except in a proceeding to determine costs. If the judgment finally obtained by the offeree is not more favorable than the offer, the offeree must pay the costs incurred after the making of the offer. The fact that an offer is made but not accepted does not preclude a subsequent offer. When the liability of one party to another has been determined by verdict or order or judgment, but the amount or extent of the liability remains to be determined by further proceedings, the party adjudged liable may make an offer of judgment, which shall have the same effect as an offer made before trial if it is served within a reasonable time not less than 10 days prior to the commencement of hearings to determine the amount or extent of liability.

As amended 1948, 1966, 1987.

APPENDIX D

STANDARDS OF PRACTICE FOR LAWYER MEDIATORS IN FAMILY DISPUTES

(Adopted by the House of Delegates of the ABA, 1984).

Preamble

For the purposes of these standards, family mediation is defined as a process in which a lawyer helps family members resolve their disputes in an informative and consensual manner. This process requires that the mediator be qualified by training, experience and temperament; that the mediator be impartial; that the participants reach decisions voluntarily; that their decisions be based on sufficient factual data; and that each participant understands the information upon which decisions are reached. While family mediation may be viewed as an alternative means of conflict resolution, it is not a substitute for the benefit of independent legal advice.

I. The Mediator Has a Duty to Define and Describe the Process of Mediation and Its Cost Before the Parties Reach an Agreement to Mediate.

Specific Considerations

Before the actual mediation sessions begin, the mediator shall conduct an orientation session to give an overview of the process and to assess the appropriateness of mediation for the participants. Among the topics covered, the mediator shall discuss the following:

(A) The mediator shall define the process in context so that the participants understand the differences between mediation and other means of conflict resolution available to them. In defining the process, the mediator shall also distinguish it from therapy or marriage counselling.

(B) The mediator shall obtain sufficient information from the participants so they can mutually define the issues to be resolved in mediation.

(C) It should be emphasized that the mediator may make suggestions for the participants to consider, such as alternative ways of resolving problems, and may draft proposals for the participants' consideration, but that all decisions are to be made voluntarily by the participants themselves, and the mediator's views are to be given no independent weight or credence.

(D) The duties and responsibilities that the mediator and the participants accept in the mediation process shall be agreed upon. The mediator shall instruct the participants that either of them or the mediator has the right to suspend or terminate the process at any time.

(E) The mediator shall assess the ability and willingness of the participants to mediate. The mediator has a continuing duty to assess his or her own ability and willingness to undertake mediation with the particular participants and the issues to be mediated. The mediator shall not continue and shall terminate the process, if in his or her judgment, one of the parties is not able or willing to participate in good faith.

(F) The mediator shall explain the fees for mediation. It is inappropriate for a mediator to charge a contingency fee or to base the fee on the outcome of the mediation process.

(G) The mediator shall inform the participants of the need to employ independent legal counsel for advice throughout the mediation process. The mediator shall inform the participants that the mediator cannot represent either or both of them in a marital dissolution or in any legal action.

(H) The mediator shall discuss the issue of separate sessions. The mediator shall reach an understanding with the participants as to whether and under what circumstances the mediator may meet alone with either of them or with any third party. Commentary: The mediator cannot act as lawyer for either party or for them jointly and should make that clear to both parties.

(I) It should be brought to the participants' attention that emotions play a part in the decision-making process. The mediator shall attempt to elicit from each of the participants a confirmation that each understands the connection between one's own emotions and the bargaining process.

II. The Mediator Shall Not Voluntarily Disclose Information Obtained Through the Mediation Process Without the Prior Consent of Both Participants.

Specific Considerations

(A) At the outset of mediation, the parties should agree in writing not to require the mediator to disclose to any party any statements made in the course of mediation. The mediator shall inform the participants that the mediator will not voluntarily disclose to any third party any of the information obtained through the mediation process, unless such disclosure is required by law, without the prior consent of the participants. The mediator also shall inform the parties of the limitations of confidentiality such as statutory or judicially mandated reporting.

(B) If subpoenaed or otherwise noticed to testify, the mediator shall inform the participants immediately so as to afford them an opportunity to quash the process.

(C) The mediator shall inform the participants of the mediator's inability to bind third parties to an agreement not to disclose information furnished during the mediation in the absence of any absolute privilege.

III. The Mediator Has a Duty to Be Impartial.

Specific Considerations

(A) The mediator shall not represent either party during or after the mediation process in any legal matters. In the event the mediator has represented one of the parties beforehand, the mediator shall not undertake the mediation.

(B) The mediator shall disclose to the participants any biases or strong views relating to the issues to be mediated, both in the orientation session, and also before these issues are discussed in mediation.

(C) The mediator must be impartial as between the mediation participants. The mediator's task is to facilitate the ability of the participants to negotiate their own agreement, while raising questions as to the fairness, equity and feasibility of proposed options for settlement.

(D) The mediator has a duty to ensure that the participants consider fully the best interests of the children, that they understand the consequences of any decision they reach concerning the children. The mediator also has a duty to assist parents to examine the separate and individual needs of their children and to consider those needs apart from their own desires for any particular parenting formula. If the mediator believes that any proposed agreement of the parents does not protect the best interests of the children, the mediator has a duty to inform them of this belief and its basis.

(E) The mediator shall not communicate with either party alone or with any third party to discuss mediation issues without the prior consent of the mediation participants. The mediator shall obtain an agreement from the participants during the orientation session as to whether and under what circumstances the mediator may speak directly and separately with each of their lawyers during the mediation process.

IV. The Mediator Has a Duty to Assure That the Mediation Participants Make Decisions Based Upon Sufficient Information and Knowledge.

Specific Considerations

(A) The mediator shall assure that there is full financial disclosure, evaluation and development of relevant factual information in the mediation process, such as each would reasonably receive in the discovery process, or that the parties have sufficient information to intelligently waive the right to such disclosure.

(B) In addition to requiring this disclosure, evaluation and development of information, the mediator shall promote the equal understanding of such information before any agreement is reached. This consideration may require the mediator to recommend that either or both obtain expert consultation in the event that it appears that additional knowledge or understanding is necessary for balanced negotiations.

(C) The mediator may define the legal issues, but shall not direct the decision of the mediation participants based upon the mediator's interpretation of the law as applied to the facts of the situation. The mediator shall endeavor to assure that the participants have a sufficient understanding of appropriate statutory and case law as well as local judicial tradition, before reaching an agreement by recommending to the participants that they obtain independent legal representation during the process.

V. The Mediator Has a Duty to Suspend or Terminate Mediation Whenever Continuation of the Process Would Harm One or More of the Participants.

Specific Considerations

(A) If the mediator believes that the participants are unable or unwilling to meaningfully participate in the process or that reasonable agreement is unlikely, the mediator may suspend or terminate mediation and should encourage the parties to seek appropriate professional help. The mediator shall recognize that the decisions are to be made by the parties on the basis of adequate information. The mediator shall not, however, participate in a process that the mediator believes will result in harm to a participant.

(B) The mediator shall assure that each person has had the opportunity to understand fully the implications and ramifications of all options available.

(C) The mediator has a duty to assure a balanced dialogue and must attempt to diffuse any manipulative or intimidating negotiation techniques utilized by either of the participants.

(D) If the mediator has suspended or terminated the process, the mediator should suggest that the participants obtain additional professional services as may be appropriate.

VI. The Mediator Has a Continuing Duty to Advise Each of the Mediation Participants to Obtain Legal Review Prior to Reaching Any Agreement.

Specific Considerations

(A) Each of the mediation participants should have independent legal counsel before reaching final agreement. At the beginning of the mediation process, the mediator should inform the participants that each should employ independent legal counsel for advice at the beginning of the process and that the independent legal counsel should be utilized throughout the process and before the participants have reached any accord to which they have made an emotional commitment.

In order to promote the integrity of the process, the mediator shall not refer either of the participants to any particular lawyers. When an attorney referral is requested, the parties should be referred to a Bar Association list if available. In the absence of such a list, the mediator may only provide a list of qualified family law attorneys in the community.

(B) The mediator shall inform the participants that the mediator cannot represent either or both of them in a marital dissolution.

(C) The mediator shall obtain an agreement from the husband and wife that each lawyer, upon request, shall be entitled to review all the factual documentation provided by the participants in the mediation process.

(D) Any memo of understanding or proposed agreement which is prepared in the mediation process should be separately reviewed by independent counsel for each participant before it is signed. While a mediator cannot insist that each participant have separate counsel, they should be discouraged from signing any agreement which has not been so reviewed. If the participants, or either of them, choose to proceed without independent counsel, the mediator shall warn them of any risk involved in not being represented, including where appropriate, the possibility that the agreement they submit to a court may be rejected as unreasonable in light of both parties' legal rights or may not be binding on them.

APPENDIX E

MANDATED PARTICIPATION AND SETTLEMENT COERCION: DISPUTE RESOLUTION AS IT RELATES TO THE COURTS

Report # 1 of the Law and Public Policy Committee of the Society of Professionals in Dispute Resolution

Approved by the Board of Directors of the Society of Professionals in Dispute Resolution on January 5, 1991

EXECUTIVE SUMMARY

Some jurisdictions by statute, rule of procedure, or court rule have required participation in dispute resolution processes such as mediation, summary jury trials, and court-annexed arbitration. The imposition of compulsory participation reflects views by legislatures or courts that benefits accrue to the courts, parties, and/or public when the use of dispute resolution procedures is not restricted to cases in which all parties agree to participate. As the use of mandatory dispute resolution has expanded, a variety of public policy issues have emerged.

The Society of Professionals in Dispute Resolution (SPIDR) and others in the field have a valuable role to play in helping to promote thoughtful and consistent public policies on these important issues. The purpose of this report is to examine the benefits and possible disadvantages of mandated participation and settlement coercion [1] and to make recommendations to policymakers. This Executive Summary of the recommendations is followed by a more extensive explanation.

Mandating participation in non-binding dispute resolution processes often is appropriate. However, compulsory programs should be carefully designed to reflect a variety of important concerns. These concerns include the monetary and emotional costs for the parties, as well as the interests of the parties in achieving results that suit their needs and that will last; the justice system's ability to deliver results that do not harm the interests of those groups that have historically operated at a disadvantage in this society; the need to have courts that function efficiently and effectively; the importance of the public's trust in the justice system; the interests of non-parties whose lives are affected and sometimes disrupted by litigation; [2] the importance of the courts' development of legal

1. The Committee uses the term settlement "coercion" to refer to the requirements added to compulsory dispute resolution processes (as distinguished from the settlement pressure normally exerted during litigation even when dispute resolution is not mandatory by the cost of litigation, the desire to avoid publicity, and other forces.) (See p. 6.)

2. For example, some might argue that the public interest in decreasing disruption in the lives of children may be served by mandating mediation of child custody disputes, even if the divorcing parents would prefer to prolong the litigation and the court would not realize savings.

precedent; and the general interest in maximizing party choice. In weighing these valid and sometimes competing concerns, policymakers should be cautious not to give undue emphasis to the desire to facilitate the efficient administration of court business and thereby subordinate other important interests. Participation should be mandated only when the compulsory program is more likely to serve these broad interests of parties, the justice system, and the public, than would procedures that would be used absent mandatory dispute resolution. (See Recommendation 1.)

Mandatory dispute resolution raises different issues than dispute resolution chosen by the parties and should be imposed only when the following criteria are met:

1. The funding for mandatory dispute resolution programs is provided on a basis comparable to funding for trials. (See Recommendation 2.)

2. Coercion to settle in the form of reports to the trier of fact and of financial disincentives to trial is not used in connection with mandated mediation. In connection with court-annexed arbitration, the financial disincentives, if any, are clear, commensurate with the interests at stake, and used only when the parties can afford to risk their imposition and proceed to trial. (See Recommendation 3.)

3. Mandatory participation is used only when a high quality program (i) is readily accessible, (ii) permits party participation, (iii) permits lawyer

participation when the parties wish it, and (iv) provides clarity about the precise procedures that are being required. (See Recommendation 4.)

In addition, the following practices should be used in connection with mandatory programs:

1. Plans for mandated dispute resolution programs should be formed in consultation with judges, other court officials, lawyers, and other dispute resolution professionals, as well as representatives of the public. Mandatory programs should be monitored to insure that they constitute an improvement over existing procedures, using criteria listed in Recommendation 1. The programs should be altered or discontinued when appropriate. (See Recommendation 5.)

2. Procedures for compulsory referrals should include, to the extent feasible, case assessment by a person knowledgeable about dispute resolution procedures and should provide for timely consideration of motions for exclusion. (See Recommendation 6.)

3. Requirements for participation and sanctions for noncompliance should be clearly defined. (See Recommendation 7.)

APPENDIX F

ETHICAL STANDARDS OF PROFESSIONAL RESPONSIBILITY FOR THE SOCIETY OF PROFESSIONALS IN DISPUTE RESOLUTION

(Adopted by the Board of Directors, June 2, 1986)

INTRODUCTION

The Society for Professionals in Dispute Resolution was established in 1973 to promote the peaceful resolution of disputes. Members of the society believe that resolving disputes through negotiation, mediation, arbitration and other neutral interventions can be of great benefit to disputing parties and to society. In 1983 the SPIDR Board charged the Ethics Committee with the task of developing ethical standards of professional responsibility. The Committee membership represented all the various sectors and disciplines within SPIDR. This document, adopted by the Board on June 2, 1986 is the result of that charge.

The purpose of this document is to promote among SPIDR members and associates ethical conduct and a high level of competency among SPIDR members, including honesty, integrity, impartiality, and the exercise of good judgment in their dispute resolution efforts. It is hoped that this document also will help to (1) define the profession of dispute resolution, (2) educate the public and (3) inform users of dispute resolution services.

Application of Standards

Adherence to these ethical standards by SPIDR members and associates is basic to professional responsibility. SPIDR members and associates commit themselves to be guided in their professional conduct by these standards. The SPIDR Board of Directors or its designee is available to advise members and associates about interpretation of these standards. Other neutral practitioners and organizations are welcome to follow these standards.

Scope

It is recognized that SPIDR members and associates resolve disputes in various sectors within the disciplines of dispute resolution and have their own codes of professional conduct. These standards have been developed as general guidelines of practice for neutral disciplines represented in the SPIDR membership. Ethical considerations relevant to some, but not to all, of these disciplines are not covered by these standards.

ETHICAL STANDARDS OF PROFESSIONAL RESPONSIBILITY FOR THE SOCIETY OF PROFESSIONALS IN DISPUTE RESOLUTION

General Responsibilities

Neutrals have a duty to the parties, to the profession, and to themselves. They should be honest and unbiased, act in good faith, be diligent, and not seek to advance their own interests at the expense of the parties.

Neutrals must act fairly in dealing with the parties, have no personal interest in the terms of the settlement, show no bias toward individuals and institutions involved in the dispute, be reasonably available as requested by the parties, and be certain that the parties are informed of the process in which they are involved.

Responsibilities to the Parties

1. *Impartiality.* The neutral must maintain impartiality toward all parties. Impartiality means freedom from favoritism or bias either by word or by action, and a commitment to serve all parties as opposed to a single party.

2. *Informed Consent.* The neutral has an obligation to assure that all parties understand the nature of the process, the procedures, the particular role of the neutral, and the parties' relationship to the neutral.

3. *Confidentiality.* Maintaining confidentiality is critical to the dispute resolution process. Confi-

dentiality encourages candor, a full exploration of the issues and a neutral's acceptability. There may be some types of cases, however, in which confidentiality is not protected. In such cases, the neutral must advise the parties, when appropriate in the dispute resolution process, that the confidentiality of the proceedings cannot necessarily be maintained. Except in such instances, the neutral must resist all attempts to cause him or her to reveal any information outside the process. A commitment by the neutral to hold information in confidence within the process also must be honored.

4. *Conflict of Interest.* The neutral must refrain from entering or continuing in any dispute if he or she believes or perceives that participation as a neutral would be a clear conflict of interest. The neutral also must disclose any circumstance that may create or give the appearance of a conflict of interest and any circumstance that may reasonably raise a question as to the neutral's impartiality.

The duty to disclose is a continuing obligation throughout the process.

5. *Promptness.* The neutral shall exert every effort to expedite the process.

6. *The Settlement and Its Consequences.* The dispute resolution process belongs to the parties. The neutral has no vested interest in the terms of a settlement, but must be satisfied that agreements in which he or she has participated will not im-

pugn the integrity of the process. The neutral has a responsibility to see that the parties consider the terms of a settlement. If the neutral is concerned about the possible consequences of a proposed agreement, and the needs of the parties dictate, the neutral must inform the parties of that concern. In adhering to this standard the neutral may find it advisable to educate the parties, to refer one or more parties for specialized advice, or to withdraw from the case. In no case, however, shall the neutral violate section 3 above, Confidentiality, of these standards.

Unrepresented Interests

The neutral must consider circumstances where interests are not represented in the process. The neutral has an obligation, where in his or her judgment the needs of the parties dictate, to assure that such interests have been considered by the principal parties.

Use of Multiple Procedures

The use of more than one dispute resolution procedure by the same neutral involves additional responsibilities. Where the use of more than one procedure is initially contemplated, the neutral must take care at the outset to advise the parties of the nature of the procedures and the consequences of revealing information during any one procedure which the neutral may later use for decision making or may share with another decision maker. Where the use of more than one procedure is contemplated after the initiation of the dispute resolution process, the neutral must explain the consequences and afford the parties an opportunity to select another neutral for the subsequent procedures. It is also incumbent upon the neutral to advise the parties of the transition from one dispute resolution process to another.

Background and Qualification

A neutral should accept responsibility only in cases where the neutral has sufficient knowledge regarding the appropriate process and subject matter to be effective. A neutral has a responsibility to maintain and improve his or her professional skills.

Disclosure of Fees

It is the duty of the neutral to explain to the parties at the outset of the process, the bases of compensation, fees and charges, if any.

Support of the Profession

The experienced neutral should participate in the development of new practitioners in the field and engage in efforts to educate the public about the value and use of neutral dispute resolution procedures. The neutral should provide *pro bono* services, as appropriate.

Responsibilities of Neutrals Working on the Same Case

In the event that more than one neutral is involved in the resolution of a dispute, each has an obligation to inform the others regarding his or her entry in the case. Neutrals working with the same parties should maintain an open and professional relationship with each other.

Advertising & Solicitation

A neutral must be aware that some forms of advertising and solicitation are inappropriate and in some conflict resolution disciplines, such as labor arbitration, are impermissible. All advertising must honestly represent the services to be rendered. No claims of specific results or promises which imply favor of one side over another for the purpose of obtaining business should be made. No commissions, rebates or other similar forms of remuneration should be given or received by a neutral for the referral of clients.

APPENDIX G

THE UNIFORM ARBITRATION ACT

[ACT RELATING TO ARBITRATION AND TO
MAKE UNIFORM THE LAW WITH
REFERENCE THERETO]

Section 1. (*Validity of Arbitration Agreement.*)

A written agreement to submit any existing controversy to arbitration or a provision in a written contract to submit to arbitration any controversy thereafter arising between the parties is valid, enforceable and irrevocable, save upon such grounds as exist at law or in equity for the revocation of any contract. This act also applies to arbitration agreements between employers and employees or between their respective representatives (unless otherwise provided in the agreement).

Section 2. (*Proceedings to Compel or Stay Arbitration.*)

(a) On application of a party showing an agreement described in Section 1, and the opposing party's refusal to arbitrate, the Court shall order the parties to proceed with arbitration, but if the opposing party denies the existence of the agreement to arbitrate, the Court shall proceed summarily to the determination of the issue raised and shall order arbitration if found for the moving party, otherwise, the application shall be denied.

(b) On application, the court may stay an arbitration proceeding commenced or threatened on a showing that there is no agreement to arbitrate. Such an issue, when in substantial and bona fide dispute, shall be forthwith and summarily tried and the stay ordered if found for the moving party. If found for the opposing party, the court shall order the parties to proceed to arbitration.

(c) If an issue referable to arbitration under the alleged agreement is involved in an action or proceeding pending in a court having jurisdiction to hear applications under subdivision (a) of this Section, the application shall be made therein. Otherwise and subject to Section 18, the application may be made in any court of competent jurisdiction.

(d) Any action or proceeding involving an issue subject to arbitration shall be stayed if an order for arbitration or an application therefor has been made under this section or, if the issue is severable, the stay may be with respect thereto only. When the application is made in such action or proceeding, the order for arbitration shall include such stay.

(e) An order for arbitration shall not be refused on the ground that the claim in issue lacks merit or bona fides or because any fault or grounds for the claim sought to be arbitrated have not been shown.

Section 3. (*Appointment of Arbitrators by Court.*)

If the arbitration agreement provides a method of appointment of arbitrators, this method shall be followed. In the absence thereof, or if the agreed method fails or for any reason cannot be followed, or when an arbitrator appointed fails or is unable to act and his successor has not been duly appointed, the court on application of a party shall appoint one or more arbitrators. An arbitrator so appointed has all the powers of one specifically named in the agreement.

Section 4. (*Majority Action by Arbitrators.*)

The powers of the arbitrators may be exercised by a majority unless otherwise provided by the agreement or by this act.

Section 5. (*Hearing.*)

Unless otherwise provided by the agreement:

(a) The arbitrators shall appoint a time and place for the hearing and cause notification to the parties to be served personally or by registered mail not less than five days before the hearing. Appearance at the hearing waives such notice. The arbitrators may adjourn the hearing from time to time as necessary and, on request of a party and for good cause, or upon their own motion may postpone the hearing to a time not later than the date fixed by the agreement for making the award unless the parties consent to a later date. The arbitrators may hear and determine the controversy upon the evidence produced notwithstanding the failure of a party duly notified to appear. The court on application may direct the arbitrators to proceed promptly with the hearing and determination of the controversy.

(b) The parties are entitled to be heard, to present evidence material to the controversy and to cross-examine witnesses appearing at the hearing.

(c) The hearing shall be conducted by all the arbitrators but a majority may determine any question and render a final award. If, during the course of the hearing, an arbitrator for any reason ceases to act, the remaining arbitrator or arbitrators appointed to act as neutrals may continue with the hearing and determination of the controversy.

Section 6.   (*Representation by Attorney.*)

A party has the right to be represented by an attorney at any proceeding or hearing under this act. A waiver thereof prior to the proceeding or hearing is ineffective.

Section 7.   (*Witnesses, Subpoenas, Depositions.*)

(a) The arbitrators may issue (cause to be issued) subpoenas for the attendance of witnesses and for the production of books, records, documents and other evidence, and shall have the power to administer oaths. Subpoenas so issued shall be served, and upon application to the Court by a party or the arbitrators, enforced, in the manner provided by law for the service and enforcement of subpoenas in a civil action.

(b) On application of a party and for use as evidence, the arbitrators may permit a deposition to be taken, in the manner and upon the terms designated by the arbitrators, of a witness who cannot be subpoenaed or is unable to attend the hearing.

(c) All provisions of law compelling a person under subpoena to testify are applicable.

(d) Fees for attendance as a witness shall be the same as for a witness in the _____ Court.

Section 8. (*Award.*)

(a) The award shall be in writing and signed by the arbitrators joining in the award. The arbitrators shall deliver a copy to each party personally or by registered mail, or as provided in the agreement.

(b) An award shall be made within the time fixed therefor by the agreement or, if not so fixed, within such time as the court orders on application of a party. The parties may extend the time in writing either before or after the expiration thereof. A party waives the objection that an award was not made within the time required unless he notifies the arbitrators of his objection prior to the delivery of the award to him.

Section 9. (*Change of Award by Arbitrators.*)

On application of a party or, if an application to the court is pending under Sections 11, 12 or 13, on submission to the arbitrators by the court under such conditions as the court may order, the arbitrators may modify or correct the award upon the grounds stated in paragraphs (1) and (3) of subdivision (a) of Section 13, or for the purpose of clarifying the award. The application shall be made within twenty days after delivery of the award to the applicant. Written notice thereof shall be given forthwith to the opposing party, stating he must serve his objections thereto, if any, within ten days from the notice. The award so modified or corrected is subject to the provisions of Sections 11, 12 and 13.

Section 10. (*Fees and Expenses of Arbitration.*)

Unless otherwise provided in the agreement to arbitrate, the arbitrators' expenses and fees, together with other expenses, not including counsel fees, incurred in the conduct of the arbitration, shall be paid as provided in the award.

Section 11. (*Confirmation of an Award.*)

Upon application of a party, the Court shall confirm an award, unless within the time limits hereinafter imposed grounds are urged for vacating or modifying or correcting the award, in which case the court shall proceed as provided in Sections 12 and 13.

Section 12. (*Vacating an Award.*)

(a) Upon application of a party, the court shall vacate an award where:

(1) The award was procured by corruption, fraud or other undue means;

(2) There was evident partiality by an arbitrator appointed as a neutral or corruption in any of the arbitrators or misconduct prejudicing the rights of any party;

(3) The arbitrators exceeded their powers;

(4) The arbitrators refused to postpone the hearing upon sufficient cause being shown therefor or refused to hear evidence material to the controversy or otherwise so conducted the hearing, contrary to the provisions of Section 5, as to prejudice substantially the rights of a party; or

(5) There was no arbitration agreement and the issue was not adversely determined in proceedings under Section 2 and the party did not participate in the arbitration hearing without raising the objection;

But the fact that the relief was such that it could not or would not be granted by a court of law or equity is not ground for vacating or refusing to confirm the award.

(b) An application under this Section shall be made within ninety days after delivery of a copy of the award to the applicant, except that, if predicated upon corruption, fraud or other undue means, it shall be made within ninety days after such grounds are known or should have been known.

(c) In vacating the award on grounds other than stated in clause (5) of Subsection (a) the court may order a rehearing before new arbitrators chosen as provided in the agreement, or in the absence thereof, by the court in accordance with Section 3, or, if the award is vacated on grounds set forth in clauses (3), and (4) of Subsection (a) the court may order a rehearing before the arbitrators who made the award or their successors appointed in accordance with Section 3. The time within which the agreement requires the award to be made is applicable to the rehearing and commences from the date of the order.

(d) If the application to vacate is denied and no motion to modify or correct the award is pending, the court shall confirm the award.

Section 13. (*Modification or Correction of Award.*)

(a) Upon application made within ninety days after delivery of a copy of the award to the applicant, the court shall modify or correct the award where:

(1) There was an evident miscalculation of figures or an evident mistake in the description of any person, thing or property referred to in the award;

(2) The arbitrators have awarded upon a matter not submitted to them and the award may be corrected without affecting the merits of the decision upon the issues submitted; or

(3) The award is imperfect in a matter of form, not affecting the merits of the controversy.

(b) If the application is granted, the court shall modify and correct the award so as to effect its intent and shall confirm the award as so modified and corrected. Otherwise, the court shall confirm the award as made.

(c) An application to modify or correct an award may be joined in the alternative with an application to vacate the award.

Section 14.   (*Judgment or Decree on Award.*)

Upon the granting of an order confirming, modifying or correcting an award, judgment or decree shall be entered in conformity therewith and be enforced as any other judgment or decree. Costs of the application and of the proceedings subsequent thereto, and disbursements may be awarded by the court.

* [Section 15.   (*Judgment Roll, Docketing.*)

(a) On entry of judgment or decree, the clerk shall prepare the judgment roll consisting, to the extent filed, of the following:

(1) The agreement and each written extension of the time within which to make the award;

(2) The award;

(3) A copy of the order confirming, modifying or correcting the award; and

(4) A copy of the judgment or decree.

* Brackets and parentheses enclose language which the Commissioners suggest may be used by those States desiring to do so.

(b) The judgment or decree may be docketed as if rendered in an action.]

Section 16. (*Applications to Court.*)

Except as otherwise provided, an application to the court under this act shall be by motion and shall be heard in the manner and upon the notice provided by law or rule of court for the making and hearing of motions. Unless the parties have agreed otherwise, notice of an initial application for an order shall be served in the manner provided by law for the service of a summons in an action.

Section 17. (*Court, Jurisdiction.*)

The term "court" means any court of competent jurisdiction of this State. The making of an agreement described in Section 1 providing for arbitration in this State confers jurisdiction on the court to enforce the agreement under this Act and to enter judgment on an award thereunder.

Section 18. (*Venue.*)

An initial application shall be made to the court of the (county) in which the agreement provides the arbitration hearing shall be held or, if the hearing has been held, in the county in which it was held. Otherwise the application shall be made in the (county) where the adverse party resides or has a place of business or, if he has no residence or place of business in this State, to the court of any (county). All subsequent applications shall be made to the court hearing the initial application unless the court otherwise directs.

Section 19. (*Appeals.*)

(a) An appeal may be taken from:

(1) An order denying an application to compel arbitration made under Section 2;

(2) An order granting an application to stay arbitration made under Section 2(b);

(3) An order confirming or denying confirmation of an award;

(4) An order modifying or correcting an award;

(5) An order vacating an award without directing a rehearing; or

(6) A judgment or decree entered pursuant to the provisions of this act.

(b) The appeal shall be taken in the manner and to the same extent as from orders or judgments in a civil action.

Section 20. (*Act Not Retroactive.*)

This act applies only to agreements made subsequent to the taking effect of this act.

Section 21. (*Uniformity of Interpretation.*)

This act shall be so construed as to effectuate its general purpose to make uniform the law of those states which enact it.

Section 22. (*Constitutionality.*)

If any provision of this act or the application thereof to any person or circumstance is held invalid, the invalidity shall not affect other provisions or applications of the act which can be given without the invalid provision or application, and to this end the provisions of this act are severable.

Section 23.   (*Short title.*)

This act may be cited as the Uniform Arbitration Act.

Section 24.   (*Repeal.*)

All acts or parts of acts which are inconsistent with the provisions of this act are hereby repealed.

Section 25.   (*Time of Taking Effect.*)

This act shall take effect _____.

APPENDIX H

FEDERAL ARBITRATION ACT

(FORMERLY UNITED STATES ARBITRATION ACT)

9 U.S.C. § 1 (1925)

Arbitration

CHAPTER 1. GENERAL PROVISIONS

Sec.
1. "Maritime Transactions," and "Commerce" Defined; Exceptions to Operation of Title.
2. Validity, Irrevocability, and Enforcement of Agreements to Arbitrate.
3. Stay of Proceedings Where Issue Therein Referable to Arbitration.
4. Failure to Arbitrate Under Agreement; Petition to United States Court Having Jurisdiction for Order to Compel Arbitration; Notice and Service Thereof; Hearing and Determination.
5. Appointment of Arbitrators or Umpire.
6. Application Heard as Motion.
7. Witnesses Before Arbitrators; Fees; Compelling Attendance.
8. Proceedings Begun by Libel in Admiralty and Seizure of Vessel or Property.
9. Award of Arbitrators; Confirmation; Jurisdiction; Procedure.
10. Same; Vacation; Grounds; Rehearing.
11. Same; Modification or Correction; Grounds; Order.

CHAPTER 1. GENERAL PROVISIONS

§ 1. "Maritime Transactions," and "Commerce" Defined; Exceptions to Operation of Title

"Maritime transactions", as herein defined, means charter parties, bills of lading of water carriers, agreements relating to wharfage, supplies furnished vessels or repairs to vessels, collisions, or any other matters in foreign commerce which, if the subject of controversy, would be embraced within admiralty jurisdiction; "commerce", as herein defined, means commerce among the several States or with foreign nations, or in any Territory of the United States or in the District of Columbia, or between any such Territory and another, or between any such Territory and any State or foreign nation, or between the District of Columbia and any State or Territory or foreign nation, but nothing herein contained shall apply to contracts of employment of seamen, railroad employees, or any other class of workers engaged in foreign or interstate commerce.

§ 2. Validity, Irrevocability, and Enforcement of Agreements to Arbitrate

A written provision in any maritime transaction or a contract evidencing a transaction involving commerce to settle by arbitration a controversy thereafter arising out of such contract or transaction, or the refusal to perform the whole or any part thereof, or an agreement in writing to submit to arbitration an existing controversy arising out of such a contract, transaction, or refusal, shall be valid, irrevocable, and enforceable, save upon such grounds as exist at law or in equity for the revocation of any contract.

§ 3. Stay of Proceedings Where Issue Therein Referable to Arbitration

If any suit or proceeding be brought in any of the courts of the United States upon any issue referable to arbitration under an agreement in writing for such arbitration, the court in which such suit is pending, upon being satisfied that the issue involved in such suit or proceeding is referable to arbitration under such an agreement, shall on application of one of the parties stay the trial of the action until such arbitration has been had in accordance with the terms of the agreement, providing the applicant for the stay is not in default in proceeding with such arbitration.

§ 4. Failure to Arbitrate Under Agreement; Petition to United States Court Having Jurisdiction for Order to Compel Arbitration; Notice and Service Thereof; Hearing and Determination

A party aggrieved by the alleged failure, neglect, or refusal of another to arbitrate under a written agreement for arbitration may petition any United States district court which, save for such agreement, would have jurisdiction under Title 28, in a civil action or in admiralty of the subject matter of a suit arising out of the controversy between the parties, for an order directing that such arbitration proceed in the manner provided for in such agreement. Five days' notice in writing of such application shall be served upon the party in default. Service thereof shall be made in the manner provided by the Federal Rules of Civil Procedure. The court shall hear the parties, and upon being satisfied that the making of the agreement for arbitration or the failure to comply therewith is not in issue, the court shall make an order directing the parties to proceed to arbitration in accordance with the terms of the agreement. The hearing and proceedings, under such agreement, shall be within the district in which the petition for an order directing such arbitration is filed. If the making of the arbitration agreement or the failure, neglect, or refusal to perform the same be in issue, the court shall proceed summarily to the trial thereof. If no jury trial be demanded by the party alleged to be in default, or if the matter in dispute is within admiralty jurisdiction, the court shall hear and determine such issue. Where such an issue is raised, the party alleged to be in default may, except in cases of admiralty, on or before the return day of the notice of application, demand a jury trial of such issue, and upon such demand the court shall make an order referring the issue or issues to a jury in the manner provided by the Federal Rules of Civil Procedure, or may specially call a jury for that purpose. If the jury find that no agreement in writing for arbitration was made or that there is no default in proceeding thereunder, the proceeding shall be dismissed. If the jury find that an agreement for arbitration was made in writing and that there is a default in proceeding thereunder, the court shall make an order summarily directing the parties to proceed with the arbitration in accordance with the terms thereof.

§ 5. Appointment of Arbitrators or Umpire

If in the agreement provision be made for a method of naming or appointing an arbitrator or arbitrators or an umpire, such method shall be followed; but if no method be provided therein, or if a method be provided and any party thereto shall fail to avail himself of such method, or if for any other reason there shall be a lapse in the naming of an arbitrator or arbitrators or umpire, or in filling a vacancy, then upon the application of either party to the controversy the court shall designate and appoint an arbitrator or arbitrators or umpire, as the case may require, who shall act under the said agreement with the same force and effect as if he or they had been specifically named therein; and unless otherwise provided in the agreement the arbitration shall be by a single arbitrator.

§ 6. Application Heard as Motion

Any application to the court hereunder shall be made and heard in the manner provided by law for the making and hearing of motions, except as otherwise herein expressly provided.

§ 7. Witnesses Before Arbitrators; Fees; Compelling Attendance

The arbitrators selected either as prescribed in this title or otherwise, or a majority of them, may summon in writing any person to attend before them or any of them as a witness and in a proper case to bring with him or them any book, record, document, or paper which may be deemed material as evidence in the case. The fees for such attendance shall be the same as the fees of witnesses before masters of the United States courts. Said summons shall issue in the name of the arbitrator or arbitrators, or a majority of them, and shall be signed by the arbitrators, or a majority of them, and shall be directed to the said person and shall be served in the same manner as subpoenas to appear and testify before the court; if any person or persons so summoned to testify shall refuse or neglect to obey said summons, upon petition the United States district court for the district in which such arbitrators, or a majority of them, are sitting may compel the attendance of such person or persons before said arbitrator or arbitrators, or punish said person or persons for contempt in the same manner provided by law for securing the attendance of witnesses or their punishment for neglect or refusal to attend in the courts of the United States.

§ 8. Proceedings Begun by Libel in Admiralty and Seizure of Vessel or Property

If the basis of jurisdiction be a cause of action otherwise justiciable in admiralty, then, notwithstanding anything herein to the contrary, the party claiming to be aggrieved may begin his proceeding hereunder by libel and seizure of the vessel or other property of the other party according to the usual course of admiralty proceedings, and the court shall then have jurisdiction to direct the parties to proceed with the arbitration and shall retain jurisdiction to enter its decree upon the award.

§ 9. Award of Arbitrators; Confirmation; Jurisdiction; Procedure

If the parties in their agreement have agreed that a judgment of the court shall be entered upon the award made pursuant to the arbitration, and shall specify the court, then at any time within one year after the award is made any party to the arbitration may apply to the court so specified for an order confirming the award, and thereupon the court must grant such an order unless the award is vacated, modified, or corrected as prescribed in sections 10 and 11 of this title. If no court is specified in the agreement of the parties, then such application may be made to the United States court in and for the district within which such award was made. Notice of the application shall be served upon the adverse party, and thereupon the court shall have jurisdiction of such party as though he had appeared generally in the proceeding. If the adverse party is a resident of the district within which the award was made, such service shall be made upon the adverse party or his attorney as prescribed by law for service of notice of motion in an action in the same court. If the adverse party shall be a nonresident, then the notice of the application shall be served by the marshal of any district within which the adverse party may be found in like manner as other process of the court.

§ 10. Same; Vacation; Grounds; Rehearing

In either of the following cases the United States court in and for the district wherein the award was made may make an order vacating the award upon the application of any party to the arbitration—

(a) Where the award was procured by corruption, fraud, or undue means.

(b) Where there was evident partiality or corruption in the arbitrators, or either of them.

(c) Where the arbitrators were guilty of misconduct in refusing to postpone the hearing, upon sufficient cause shown, or in refusing to hear evidence pertinent and material to the controversy; or of any other misbehavior by which the rights of any party have been prejudiced.

(d) Where the arbitrators exceeded their powers, or so imperfectly executed them that a mutual, final, and definite award upon the subject matter submitted was not made.

(e) Where an award is vacated and the time within which the agreement required the award to be made has not expired the court may, in its discretion, direct a rehearing by the arbitrators.

§ 11. Same; Modification or Correction; Grounds; Order

In either of the following cases the United States court in and for the district wherein the award was made may make an order modifying or correcting the award upon the application of any party to the arbitration—

(a) Where there was an evident material miscalculation of figures or an evident material mistake in the description of any person, thing, or property referred to in the award.

(b) Where the arbitrators have awarded upon a matter not submitted to them, unless it is a matter not affecting the merits of the decision upon the matter submitted.

(c) Where the award is imperfect in matter of form not affecting the merits of the controversy.

The order may modify and correct the award, so as to effect the intent thereof and promote justice between the parties.

§ 12. Notice of Motions to Vacate or Modify; Service; Stay of Proceedings

Notice of a motion to vacate, modify, or correct an award must be served upon the adverse party or his attorney within three months after the award is filed or delivered. If the adverse party is a resident of the district within which the award was made, such service shall be made upon the adverse party or his attorney as prescribed by law for service of notice of motion in an action in the same court. If the adverse party shall be a nonresident then the notice of the application shall be served by the marshal of any district within which the adverse party may be found in like manner as other process of the court. For the purposes of the motion any judge who might make an order to stay the proceedings in an action brought in the same court may make an order, to be served with the notice of motion, staying the proceedings of the adverse party to enforce the award.

§ 13. Papers Filed With Order on Motions; Judgment; Docketing; Force and Effect; Enforcement

The party moving for an order confirming, modifying, or correcting an award shall, at the time such order is filed with the clerk for the entry of judgment thereon, also file the following papers with the clerk:

(a) The agreement; the selection or appointment, if any, of an additional arbitrator or umpire; and each written extension of the time, if any, within which to make the award.

(b) The award.

(c) Each notice, affidavit, or other paper used upon an application to confirm, modify, or correct the award, and a copy of each order of the court upon such an application.

The judgment shall be docketed as if it was rendered in an action.

The judgment so entered shall have the same force and effect, in all respects, as, and be subject to all the provisions of law relating to, a judgment in an action; and it may be enforced as if it had been rendered in an action in the court in which it is entered.

§ 14. Contracts Not Affected

This title shall not apply to contracts made prior to January 1, 1926.

§ 15. Inapplicability of the Act of State Doctrine

Enforcement of arbitral agreements, confirmation of arbitral awards, and execution upon judgments based on orders confirming such awards shall not be refused on the basis of the Act of State doctrine.

§ 15.[1] Appeals

(a) An appeal may be taken from—

(1) an order—

(A) refusing a stay of any action under section 3 of this title,

(B) denying a petition under section 4 of this title to order arbitration to proceed,

(C) denying an application under section 206 of this title to compel arbitration,

(D) confirming or denying confirmation of an award or partial award, or

(E) modifying, correcting, or vacating an award;

(2) an interlocutory order granting, continuing, or modifying an injunction against an arbitration that is subject to this title; or

(3) a final decision with respect to an arbitration that is subject to this title.

(b) Except as otherwise provided in section 1292(b) of title 28, an appeal may not be taken from an interlocutory order—

1. So in original. There are two sections designated "15".

(1) granting a stay of any action under section 3 of this title;

(2) directing arbitration to proceed under section 4 of this title;

(3) compelling arbitration under section 206 of this title; or

(4) refusing to enjoin an arbitration that is subject to this title.

CHAPTER 2. CONVENTION ON THE RECOGNITION AND ENFORCEMENT OF FOREIGN ARBITRAL AWARDS

§ 201. Enforcement of Convention

The Convention on the Recognition and Enforcement of Foreign Arbitral Awards of June 10, 1958, shall be enforced in United States courts in accordance with this chapter.

§ 202. Agreement or Award Falling Under the Convention

An arbitration agreement or arbitral award arising out of a legal relationship, whether contractual or not, which is considered as commercial, including a transaction, contract, or agreement described in section 2 of this title, falls under the Convention. An agreement or award arising out of such a relationship which is entirely between citizens of the United States shall be deemed not to fall under the Convention unless that relationship involves property located abroad, envisages performance or enforcement abroad, or has some other reasonable relation with one or more foreign states. For the purpose of this section a corporation is a citizen of the United States if it is incorporated or has its principal place of business in the United States.

§ 203. Jurisdiction; Amount in Controversy

An action or proceeding falling under the Convention shall be deemed to arise under the laws and treaties of the United States. The district courts of the United States (including the courts enumerated in section 460 of title 28) shall have original jurisdiction over such an action or proceeding, regardless of the amount in controversy.

§ 204. Venue

An action or proceeding over which the district courts have jurisdiction pursuant to section 203 of this title may be brought in any such court in which save for the arbitration agreement an action or proceeding with respect to the controversy between the parties could be brought, or in such court for the district and division which embraces the place designated in the agreement as the place of arbitration if such place is within the United States.

§ 205. Removal of Cases From State Courts

Where the subject matter of an action or proceeding pending in a State court relates to an arbitration agreement or award falling under the Convention, the defendant or the defendants may, at any time before the trial thereof, remove such action or proceeding to the district court of the

United States for the district and division embracing the place where the action or proceeding is pending. The procedure for removal of causes otherwise provided by law shall apply, except that the ground for removal provided in this section need not appear on the face of the complaint but may be shown in the petition for removal. For the purposes of Chapter 1 of this title any action or proceeding removed under this section shall be deemed to have been brought in the district court to which it is removed.

§ 206. Order to Compel Arbitration; Appointment of Arbitrators

A court having jurisdiction under this chapter may direct that arbitration be held in accordance with the agreement at any place therein provided for, whether that place is within or without the United States. Such court may also appoint arbitrators in accordance with the provisions of the agreement.

§ 207. Award of Arbitrators; Confirmation; Jurisdiction; Proceeding

Within three years after an arbitral award falling under the Convention is made, any party to the arbitration may apply to any court having jurisdiction under this chapter for an order confirming the award as against any other party to the arbitration. The court shall confirm the award unless it finds one of the grounds for refusal or deferral of recognition or enforcement of the award specified in the said Convention.

§ 208. Chapter 1; Residual Application

Chapter 1 applies to actions and proceedings brought under this chapter to the extent that chapter is not in conflict with this chapter or the Convention as ratified by the United States.

APPENDIX I

DEMAND FOR ARBITRATION

American Arbitration Association

MEDIATION Please consult the Commercial Mediation Rules regarding mediation procedures. If you want the A.A.A to contact the other party and attempt to arrange a mediation, please check this box. ☐

COMMERCIAL ARBITRATION RULES
DEMAND FOR ARBITRATION

DATE: _____

TO: Name _____
(of the party upon whom the demand is made)

Address _____

City and State _____ ZIP Code _____

Telephone ( ) _____ Fax _____

Name of Representative _____
(if known)

Representative's Address _____

City and State _____ ZIP Code _____

Telephone ( ) _____ Fax _____

The named claimant, a party to an arbitration agreement contained in a written contract, dated _____, providing for arbitration under the Commercial Arbitration Rules, hereby demands arbitration thereunder (attach the arbitration clause or quote it hereunder).

NATURE OF DISPUTE:

CLAIM OR RELIEF SOUGHT (amount, if any):

TYPE OF BUSINESS: Claimant _____ Respondent _____

PLEASE TAKE FURTHER NOTICE that, unless within twenty days after service of this Notice of Intention to Arbitrate you apply to stay the arbitration herein pursuant to Article 75 of the New York Civil Practice Law and Rules, you shall thereafter be precluded from objecting that a valid agreement was not made or has not been complied with and from asserting in court the bar of a limitation of time.

HEARING LOCALE REQUESTED: _____ _____
(City and State)

You are hereby notified that copies of our arbitration agreement and of this demand are being filed with the American Arbitration Association at its _____ _____ Title _____ office, with the request that it commence the administration of the arbitration. Under the rules, you may file an answering statement within seven days after notice from the administrator.

Signed _____
(may be signed by a representative)

Name of Claimant _____

Address (to be used in connection with this case) _____

City and State _____ ZIP Code _____

Telephone ( ) _____ Fax _____

Name of Representative _____

Representative's Address _____

City and State _____ ZIP Code _____

Telephone ( ) _____ Fax _____

To institute proceedings, please send three copies of this demand and the arbitration agreement, with the filing fee, as provided for in the rules, to the AAA. Send the original demand to the respondent.

[G10091] Form C2NY–1/90
FOR USE IN NEW YORK STATE

APPENDIX J

CODE OF ETHICS FOR ARBITRATORS IN COMMERCIAL DISPUTES [1]

(Issued in 1977)

Preamble

The use of commercial arbitration to resolve a wide variety of disputes has grown extensively and forms a significant part of the system of justice which our society relies upon for the fair determination of legal rights. Persons who act as commercial arbitrators therefore undertake serious responsibilities to the public as well as to the parties. These responsibilities include important ethical obligations.

Few cases of unethical behavior by commercial arbitrators have arisen. Nevertheless, the American Bar Association and the American Arbitration Association believe that it is in the public interest to set forth generally accepted standards of ethical conduct for the guidance of arbitrators and parties in commercial disputes. By establishing this Code,

1. This Code was prepared by a Joint Committee consisting of a Special Committee of the American Arbitration Association and a Special Committee of the American Bar Association. It has been approved and recommended by both organizations.

the sponsors hope to contribute to the maintenance of high standards and continued confidence in the process of arbitration.

There are many different types of commercial arbitration. Some cases are conducted under arbitration rules established by various organizations and trade associations, while others are carried on without such rules. Although most cases are arbitrated pursuant to voluntary agreement of the parties, certain types of disputes are submitted to arbitration by reason of particular laws. This Code is intended to apply to all such proceedings in which disputes or claims are submitted for decision to one or more arbitrators appointed in a manner provided by an agreement of the parties, by applicable arbitration rules or by law. In all such cases the persons who have the power to decide should observe fundamental standards of ethical conduct. In this Code all such persons are called "arbitrators," although in some types of cases they may be called "umpires" or may have some other title.

Various aspects of the conduct of arbitrators, including some matters covered by this Code, may be governed by agreements of the parties, by arbitration rules to which the parties have agreed, or by applicable law. This Code does not take the place of, or supersede, any such agreements, rules and laws and does not establish any new or additional grounds for judicial review or arbitration awards.

While this Code is intended to provide ethical guidelines in many types of arbitration, it does not form part of the arbitration rules of the American Arbitration Association or of any other organization, nor is it intended to apply to mediation or conciliation. Labor arbitrations are governed by the "Code of Professional Responsibility for Arbitrators of Labor–Management Disputes," not by this Code.

Arbitrators, like judges, have the power to decide cases. However, unlike full-time judges, arbitrators are usually engaged in other occupations before, during and after the time they serve as arbitrators. Often arbitrators are purposely chosen from the same trade or industry as the parties in order to bring special knowledge to the task of deciding. This Code recognizes these fundamental differences between arbitrators and judges.

In some types of arbitration there are three, or more, arbitrators. In these cases, it is sometimes the practice for each party, acting alone, to appoint one arbitrator and for the other arbitrator(s) to be designated by those two, or by the parties, or by an independent institution or individual. The sponsors of this Code believe that it is preferable for parties to agree that all arbitrators should comply with the same ethical standards. However, it is recognized that there is a long-established practice in some types of arbitration for those arbitrators who are appointed by one party, acting alone, to be governed by special ethical considerations. Those special considerations are set forth in the last section of the Code, headed "Ethical Considerations Relating to Arbitrators Appointed by One Party."

Although this Code is sponsored by the American Arbitration Association and the American Bar Association, its use is not limited to arbitrations administered by the AAA or to cases in which the arbitrators are lawyers. Rather, it is presented as a public service to provide guidance in all types of commercial arbitration.

Canon I. An Arbitrator Should Uphold the Integrity and Fairness of the Arbitration Process

A. Fair and just processes for resolving disputes are indispensable in our society. Commercial arbitration is an important method for deciding many types of disputes. In order for commercial arbitration to be effective, there must be broad public confidence in the integrity and fairness of the process. Therefore, an arbitrator has a responsibility not only to the parties but also to the process of arbitration itself, and must observe high standards of conduct so that the integrity and fairness of the process will be preserved. Accordingly, an arbitrator should recognize a responsibility to the public, to the parties whose rights will be decided, and to all other participants in the proceeding. The provisions of this Code should be construed and applied to further these objectives.

B. It is inconsistent with the integrity of the arbitration process for persons to solicit appointment for themselves. However, a person may indicate a general willingness to serve as an arbitrator.

C. Persons should accept appointment as arbitrators only if they believe that they can be available to conduct the arbitration promptly.

D. After accepting appointment and while serving as an arbitrator, a person should avoid entering into any financial, business, professional, family or social relationship, or acquiring any financial or personal interest, which is likely to affect impartiality or which might reasonably create the appearance of partiality or bias. For a reasonable period of time after the decision of a case, persons who have served as arbitrators should avoid entering into any such relationship, or acquiring any such interest, in circumstances which might reasonably create the appearance that they had been influenced in the arbitration by the anticipation or expectation of the relationship or interest.

E. Arbitrators should conduct themselves in a way that is fair to all parties and should not be swayed by outside pressure, by public clamor, by fear of criticism or by self-interest.

F. When an arbitrator's authority is derived from an agreement of the parties, the arbitrator should neither exceed that authority nor do less than is required to exercise that authority completely. Where the agreement of the parties sets forth procedures to be followed in conducting the arbitration or refers to rules to be followed, it is the obligation of the arbitrator to comply with such procedures or rules.

G. An arbitrator should make all reasonable efforts to prevent delaying tactics, harassment of parties or other participants, or other abuse or disruption of the arbitration process.

H. The ethical obligations of an arbitrator begin upon acceptance of the appointment and continue throughout all stages of the proceeding. In addition, wherever specifically set forth in this Code, certain ethical obligations begin as soon as a person is requested to serve as an arbitrator and certain ethical obligations continue even after the decision in the case has been given to the parties.

Canon II. An Arbitrator Should Disclose Any Interest or Relationship Likely to Affect Impartiality or Which Might Create an Appearance of Partiality or Bias

Introductory Note:

This Code reflects the prevailing principle that arbitrators should disclose the existence of any interests or relationships which are likely to affect their impartiality or which might reasonably create the appearance that they are biased against one party or favorable to another. These provisions of the Code are intended to be applied realistically so that the burden of detailed disclosure does not become so great that it is impractical for persons in the business world to be arbitrators, thereby depriving parties of the services of those who might be best informed and qualified to decide particular types of cases.

This Code does not limit the freedom of parties to agree on anyone they choose as an arbitrator. When parties, with knowledge of a person's interests and relationships, nevertheless desire that individual to serve as an arbitrator, that person may properly serve.

Disclosure:

A. Persons who are requested to serve as arbitrators should, before accepting, disclose:

(1) Any direct or indirect financial or personal interest in the outcome of the arbitration;

(2) Any existing or past financial, business, professional, family or social relationships which are likely to affect impartiality or which might reasonably create an appearance of partiality or bias. Persons requested to serve as arbitrators should disclose any such relationships which they personally have with any party or its lawyer, or with any individual whom they have been told will be a witness. They should also disclose any such relationships involving members of their families or their current employers, partners or business associates.

B. Persons who are requested to accept appointment as arbitrators should make a reasonable effort to inform themselves of any interests or relationships described in Paragraph A above.

C. The obligation to disclose interests or relationships described in Paragraph A above is a continuing duty which requires a person who accepts appointment as an arbitrator to disclose, at any stage of the arbitration, any such interests or relationships which may arise, or which are recalled or discovered.

D. Disclosure should be made to all parties unless other procedures for disclosure are provided in the rules or practices of an institution which is administering the arbitration. Where more than one arbitrator has been appointed, each should inform the others of the interests and relationships which have been disclosed.

E. In the event that an arbitrator is requested by all parties to withdraw, the arbitrator should do so. In the event that an arbitrator is requested to withdraw by less than all of the parties because of alleged partiality or bias, the arbitrator should withdraw unless either of the following circumstances exists:

(1) If an agreement of the parties, or arbitration rules agreed to by the parties, establishes procedures for determining challenges to arbitrators, then those procedures should be followed; or

(2) If the arbitrator, after carefully considering the matter, determines that the reason for the challenge is not substantial, and that he or she can nevertheless act and decide the case impartially and fairly, and that with-

drawal would cause unfair delay or expense to another party or would be contrary to the ends of justice.

Canon III. An Arbitrator in Communicating With the Parties Should Avoid Impropriety or the Appearance of Impropriety

A. If an agreement of the parties, or any applicable arbitration rules referred to in that agreement, establishes the manner or content of communications between the arbitrator and the parties, the arbitrator should follow those procedures notwithstanding any contrary provisions of the following Paragraphs B and C.

B. Unless otherwise provided in applicable arbitration rules or in an agreement of the parties, arbitrators should not discuss a case with any party in the absence of each other party, except in any of the following circumstances:

(1) Discussions may be had with a party concerning such matters as setting the time and place of hearings or making other arrangements for the conduct of the proceedings. However, the arbitrator should promptly inform each other party of the discussion and should not make any final determination concerning the matter discussed before giving each absent party an opportunity to express its views.

(2) If a party fails to be present at a hearing after having been given due notice, the arbi-

trator may discuss the case with any party who is present.

(3) If all parties request or consent that such discussion take place.

C.   Unless otherwise provided in applicable arbitration rules or in an agreement of the parties, whenever an arbitrator communicates in writing with one party, the arbitrator should at the same time send a copy of the communication to each other party.   Whenever an arbitrator receives any written communication concerning the case from one party which has not already been sent to each other party, the arbitrator should do so.

Canon IV. An Arbitrator Should Conduct the Proceedings Fairly and Diligently

A.   An arbitrator should conduct the proceedings in an evenhanded manner and treat all parties with equality and fairness at all stages of the proceedings.

B.   An arbitrator should perform duties diligently and conclude the case as promptly as the circumstances reasonably permit.

C.   An arbitrator should be patient and courteous to the parties, to their lawyers and to the witnesses and should encourage similar conduct by all participants in the proceedings.

D.   Unless otherwise agreed by the parties or provided in arbitration rules agreed to by the parties, an arbitrator should accord to all parties the right to appear in person and to be heard after due notice of the time and place of hearing.

E. An arbitrator should not deny any party the opportunity to be represented by counsel.

F. If a party fails to appear after due notice, an arbitrator should proceed with the arbitration when authorized to do so by the agreement of the parties, the rules agreed to by the parties or by law. However, an arbitrator should do so only after receiving assurance that notice has been given to the absent party.

G. When an arbitrator determines that more information than has been presented by the parties is required to decide the case, it is not improper for the arbitrator to ask questions, call witnesses, and request documents or other evidence.

H. It is not improper for an arbitrator to suggest to the parties that they discuss the possibility of settlement of the case. However, an arbitrator should not be present or otherwise participate in the settlement discussions unless requested to do so by all parties. An arbitrator should not exert pressure on any party to settle.

I. Nothing in this Code is intended to prevent a person from acting as a mediator or conciliator of a dispute in which he or she has been appointed as arbitrator, if requested to do so by all parties or where authorized or required to do so by applicable laws or rules.

J.   When there is more than one arbitrator, the arbitrators should afford each other the full opportunity to participate in all aspects of the proceedings.

Canon V.   An Arbitrator Should Make Decisions in a Just, Independent and Deliberate Manner

A.   An arbitrator should, after careful deliberation, decide all issues submitted for determination. An arbitrator should decide no other issues.

B.   An arbitrator should decide all matters justly, exercising independent judgment, and should not permit outside pressure to affect the decision.

C.   An arbitrator should not delegate the duty to decide to any other person.

D.   In the event that all parties agree upon a settlement of the issues in dispute and request an arbitrator to embody that agreement in an award, an arbitrator may do so, but is not required to do so unless satisfied with the propriety of the terms of settlement.   Whenever an arbitrator embodies a settlement by the parties in an award, the arbitrator should state in the award that it is based on an agreement of the parties.

Canon VI.   An Arbitrator Should Be Faithful to the Relationship of Trust and Confidentiality Inherent in That Office

A.   An arbitrator is in a relationship of trust to the parties and should not, at any time, use confidential information acquired during the arbitration proceeding to gain personal advantage or advantage for others, or to affect adversely the interest of another.

B.   Unless otherwise agreed by the parties, or required by applicable rules or law, an arbitrator should keep confidential all matters relating to the arbitration proceedings and decision.

C.   It is not proper at any time for an arbitrator to inform anyone of the decision in advance of the time it is given to all parties.   In a case in which there is more than one arbitrator, it is not proper at any time for an arbitrator to inform anyone concerning the deliberations of the arbitrators. After an arbitration award has been made, it is not proper for an arbitrator to assist in any post-arbitration proceedings, except as may be required by law.

D.   In many types of arbitration it is customary practice for the arbitrators to serve without pay. However, in some types of cases it is customary for arbitrators to receive compensation for their services and reimbursement for their expenses.   In cases in which any such payments are to be made, all persons who are requested to serve, or who are serving as arbitrators, should be governed by the same high standards of integrity and fairness as apply to their other activities in the case.   Accordingly, such persons should scrupulously avoid bargaining with parties over the amount of payments or engaging in any communications concerning payments which would create an appearance of coercion or other impropriety. In the absence of governing provisions in the agreement of the parties or in rules agreed to by the parties or in applicable law, certain practices relating to payments are generally recognized as being preferable in order to preserve the integrity and fairness of the arbitration process. These practices include:

(1) It is preferable that before the arbitrator finally accepts appointment the basis of payment be established and that all parties be informed thereof in writing.

(2) In cases conducted under the rules or administration of an institution which is available to assist in making arrangements for payments, the payments should be arranged by the institution to avoid the necessity for communication by the arbitrators directly with the parties concerning the subject.

(3) In cases where no institution is available to assist in making arrangements for payments, it is preferable that any discussions with arbitrators concerning payments should take place in the presence of all parties.

Canon VII. Ethical Considerations Relating to Arbitrators Appointed by One Party

Introductory Note:

In some types of arbitration in which there are three arbitrators it is customary for each party, acting alone, to appoint one arbitrator. The third arbitrator is then appointed either by agreement of the parties or of the two arbitrators, or, failing such agreement, by an independent institution or individual. In some of these types of arbitration, all three arbitrators are customarily considered to be neutral and are expected to observe the same standards of ethical conduct. However, there are also many types of tripartite arbitration in which it has been the practice that the two arbitrators appointed by the parties are not considered to be neutral and are expected to observe many—but not all—of the same ethical standards as the neutral third arbitrator. For the purposes of this Code, an arbitrator appointed by one party who is not expected to observe all of the same standards as the third arbitrator is referred to as a "non-neutral arbitrator." This Canon VII describes the ethical obligations which non-neutral party-appointed arbitrators should observe and those which are not applicable to them.

In all arbitrations in which there are two or more party-appointed arbitrators, it is important for everyone concerned to know from the start whether the party-appointed arbitrators are expected to be neutrals or non-neutrals. In such arbitrations, the two party-appointed arbitrators should be considered non-neutrals unless both parties inform the arbitrators that all three arbitrators are to be neutral, or unless the contract, the applicable arbitration rules, or any governing law requires that all three arbitrators are to be neutral.

It should be noted that in cases where the arbitration is conducted outside the United States the applicable law may require that all arbitrators be neutral. Accordingly, in such cases the governing law should be considered before applying any of the following provisions relating to non-neutral party-appointed arbitrators.

A. *Obligations Under Canon I:*

Non-neutral party-appointed arbitrators should observe all of the obligations of Canon I to uphold the integrity and fairness of the arbitration process, subject only to the following provisions:

(1) Non-neutral arbitrators may be predisposed toward the party who appointed them but in all other respects are obligated to act in good faith and with integrity and fairness. For example, non-neutral arbitrators should not engage in delaying tactics or harassment of any party or witness and should not knowingly make untrue or misleading statements to the other arbitrators.

(2) The provisions of Canon I–D relating to relationships and interests are not applicable to non-neutral arbitrators.

B. *Obligations Under Canon II:*

Non-neutral party-appointed arbitrators should disclose to all parties, and to the other arbitrators, all interests and relationships which Canon II requires be disclosed. Disclosure as required by Canon II is for the benefit not only of the party who appointed the non-neutral arbitrator, but also for the benefit of the other parties and arbitrators so that they may know of any bias which may exist or appear to exist. However, this obligation is subject to the following provisions:

(1) Disclosure by non-neutral arbitrators should be sufficient to describe the general nature and scope of any interest or relationship, but need not include as detailed information as is expected from persons appointed as neutral arbitrators.

(2) Non-neutral arbitrators are not obligated to withdraw if requested to do so by the party who did not appoint them, notwithstanding the provisions of Canon II–E.

C. *Obligations Under Canon III:*

Non-neutral party-appointed arbitrators should observe all of the obligations of Canon III concerning communications with the parties, subject only to the following provisions:

(1) In an arbitration in which the two party-appointed arbitrators are expected to appoint the third arbitrator, non-neutral arbitrators may consult with the party who appointed them concerning the acceptability of persons under consideration for appointment as the third arbitrator.

(2) Non-neutral arbitrators may communicate with the party who appointed them concerning any other aspect of the case, provided they first inform the other arbitrators and the parties that they intend to do so. If such communication occurred prior to the time the person was appointed as arbitrator, or prior to the first hearing or other meeting of the parties with the arbitrators, the non-neutral arbitrator should at the first hearing or meeting, disclose the fact that such communication has taken place. In complying with the provisions of this paragraph, it is sufficient that there be disclosure of the fact that such communication has occurred without disclosing the content of the communication. It is also sufficient to disclose at any time the intention to follow the procedure of having such communications in the future and there is no requirement thereafter that there be disclosure before each separate occasion on which such a communication occurs.

(3) When non-neutral arbitrators communicate in writing with the party who appointed them concerning any matter as to which communication is permitted under this Code, they are not required to send copies of any such written communications to any other party or arbitrator.

D. *Obligations Under Canon IV:*

Non-neutral party-appointed arbitrators should observe all of the obligations of Canon IV to conduct the proceedings fairly and diligently.

E. *Obligations Under Canon V:*

Non-neutral party-appointed arbitrators should observe all of the obligations of Canon V concerning making decisions, subject only to the following provision:

(1) Non-neutral arbitrators are permitted to be predisposed toward deciding in favor of the party who appointed them.

F. *Obligations Under Canon VI:*

Non-neutral party-appointed arbitrators should observe all of the obligations of Canon VI to be faithful to the relationship of trust inherent in the office of arbitrator, subject only to the following provision:

(1) Non-neutral arbitrators are not subject to the provisions of Canon VI–D with respect to any payments by the party who appointed them.

*

Index

References are to Pages

†